LEGAL REALISM AND JUSTICE

LEGAL REALISM AND JUSTICE

By Edwin N. Garlan

NEW YORK: MORNINGSIDE HEIGHTS
COLUMBIA UNIVERSITY PRESS
1941

Foreign Agents: Oxford University Press, Humphrey Milford, Amen House, London, E.C. 4, England, and B. I. Building, Nicol Road, Bombay, India; Maruzen Company, Ltd., 6 Nihonbashi, Tori-Nichome, Tokyo, Japan

MANUFACTURED IN THE UNITED STATES OF AMERICA

To

B. C. G.

FOREWORD

When in the course of human events an intellectual revolt acquires a name and an influential constituency, it also acquires a history and a philosophy. The movement which became vocal in the twenties and acquired a name in the thirties as American legal realism, or neorealism, is now seen to have historical continuity with the writings of earlier jurists and logical continuity within the contexts of philosophy. In this volume Garlan has admirably clarified the philosophical continuity of American legal realism. The movement has, indeed, gained sufficient influence among legal scholars, law students, judges, administrative officials, and even practitioners to make it important for an understanding of contemporary legal problems. Without trying to pass judgment on the immediate objects of some of its followers, without entering into the technical problems of law and its administration, Garlan has revealed the excesses of some of the realists, detected the genuine objectives of the movement, and shown the meaning of these objectives in the broader context of a theory of justice. In so doing, he has fulfilled the function of the philosopher as the intellectual mediator between the immediate and the enduring in experience.

With the history of American legal realism, the author has not been concerned. He has not, for example, traced the influence of the late Oliver Wendell Holmes, Jr., upon

Hohfeld and Corbin, upon Llewellyn and Frank; nor the influence of Bentham on Ihering and of Ihering on Pound; nor of all of these on Cardozo. This is a task for others; to have injected it into Garlan's analytical survey of contemporary legal realism would have confused the issues which he raises. He confines, therefore, his study of juristic writings to those of the last two or three decades and, with the possible exception of Cardozo, to those who are clearly recognized as leaders or followers of realism. His interpretations and criticisms of the writings of contemporary legal realists, while not exhaustive, are the most comprehensive and thorough which have come to my attention. The reader who wants to understand this important movement in its broad and nontechnical aspects can find no better summary in print. Moreover, the Selective Bibliography is the most comprehensive available. It includes, in addition to all the general discussions of realist theories, many articles on special legal topics which reveal the influences and methods of realism.

Nearly a decade has passed since American legal realism, or some of its outcroppings, became the subject of sharp, and even bitter, controversy in the leading law reviews. With the detachment and the tolerance which every philosopher should have, Garlan has shown in this book that American legal realism is not an integrated philosophy of law, that many of its leaders and followers have divergent or incompatible theories about law, and that some of them do not mean what they seem to say. In part he supports Professor Llewellyn's earlier contention (44 *Harvard Law Review* 1222) that there is no "school" of American legal realism. Yet Garlan has produced persuasive evidence that the American legal realists have certain common objectives and that their concern is not alone with the law that is. They are also concerned with what the law ought to be, with the theory of justice.

In his discussion of justice, Garlan is more than a reporter and a critic. He has made his own valuable contribution to problems of human conduct on which men have observed and reflected and argued at least as long as they have speculated on the problems of natural science. What that contribution is, the reader can best judge for himself. The author has no ideal code, no absolute principles of justice. There is no formula of justice; there are only "formulae." The "unity" of justice lies not in its attaining an intellectual definition but in its motive power in the minds of men. In turn, he examines "impartiality," "reasonableness," "the common good," and other ideas in the contexts of their legal application and concludes that none of them exhausts the meaning of justice. "Impartiality," for example, is too narrow and becomes the "sporting" or "umpire" theory of adjudication, which is all too prevalent in America. Other proposed equivalents serve to cover up the incompatibility of the values which ought to be detected in the course of adjudication. Justice, then, is not so much the answer to questions as the continuous questioning which evokes afresh in each case the insight into values involved in the adjustment of disputes and the awareness of the necessity of choice between incompatible values. In thus directing his attention to the judicial process, in that larger context which Cardozo gave it, Garlan has brought his own philosophy of law into focus upon the predominant theme of the American legal realists.

Edwin W. Patterson

School of Law, Columbia University
November, 1940

PREFACE

A THEORY of justice performs various functions. The functions in any given age are determined by the needs of the time. But whatever the functions are, the need to reformulate the principles by which law lives is an ever-recurring need. New insights are gained or old ones recaptured, modifications of existing habits of social and legal action are made, new objectives are formed, new conflicts emerge, and from the growing disorder of change a new ordered vision of the organizing principles of law is required. That there is a continuity with the past need hardly be argued. In fact, what so frequently appears to be a radical alteration of existing perspectives turns out on closer scrutiny to be a formulation in new language, closer perhaps to the idiom of the present, of what in its essential character is identical with men's common vision of their ends and standards. We have today an impelling need for a theory of justice which will incorporate and be adequate to our insights and activities. This book is not intended to be a complete answer to this need. The intention is to present positive suggestions and negative conclusions which are important to a theory that would express our contemporary experience.

The present work owes much to the insights into the legal process gained from a study of contemporary realistic writers in jurisprudence. Upon the methodological basis provided by a realistic approach to law I have tried to trace the implications for a theory of justice. I am convinced that legal realism is not a sect in our contemporary society of which law is a part, but rather that legal realism most nearly expresses present-day attitudes, temporary as they may possibly be. I am also convinced that legal realism is not as indifferent to the theory of justice as some would suppose.

My thanks for personal advice and encouragement are due to many, but they are due especially to Professor H. W. Schneider of the Department of Philosophy, Columbia University, and to Professors R. L. Hale, K. N. Llewellyn, and E. W. Patterson of the School of Law, Columbia University. Whatever mistakes I have managed to avoid is due in great part to their kindly criticisms and suggestions. For the opportunity and freedom to do this work at all, as well as for the friendly atmosphere in which it was done, I am deeply grateful to my brother and sister-in-law, Dr. and Mrs. S. A. Garlan.

For permission to include materials from other publications, I wish to thank the editors of the *Columbia Law Review, Harvard Law Review, University of Pennsylvania Law Review, California Law Review, Notre Dame Lawyer, Law Quarterly Review, Philosophical Review,* and *American Journal of Sociology* and the Open Court Publishing Company, Columbia University Press, Yale University Press, University of Chicago Press, Cambridge University Press, New York University Press, H. Holt and Company, and Longmans, Green and Company.

EDWIN N. GARLAN

Columbia University
November, 1940

CONTENTS

LEGAL REALISM
AND JUSTICE

CHAPTER I

INTRODUCTION

Law is by nature conservative. It crystallizes loose institutional and group habits into permanent principles of action; it forges the ways of men into stable structures which are highly resistant to change. The power of words to fix patterns of action has few better illustrations than are to be found in law. Law is considered, and not without cause, as the chief symbol and the closest embodiment of the ideals of certainty, security, and permanence, and, true to its conserving function, law responds to new forces only after the consequences of these new forces in ideas, methods, and objectives have become well articulated in other institutions and the sciences concerned with these institutions.

So it is that today men in law are still struggling against a frame of reference predicated upon premises, principles, and methods characteristic of eighteenth-century rationalism and nineteenth-century evolutionism and utilitarianism, attitudes which have already been seriously questioned and modified in other social disciplines. The shift in attitude is in the direction of a pragmatic philosophy of law. Though anticipated by many individuals and by the development of a sociological jurisprudence, the effective struggle against traditional attitudes has arisen in the United States with the emergence of a realistic jurisprudence.[1] Today the realists in contemporary American jurisprudence are providing a more concrete and practical approach to law than was afforded by a more abstract and formal jurisprudence. The center of interest for the realist is twofold: in devising an experimental and fact-controlled method and in a functional interpretation of law as an institutional process operating in the larger social matrix and tested by its contributions to the larger whole.[2]

THE REVOLT AGAINST CONCEPTUALISM

Though American legal realism is heavily influenced by contemporary intellectual currents, the pragmatic and realistic approach to law has some of its deepest roots in the practices, the insights, and the practical art of the lawyer.

[1] See Llewellyn, *A Realistic Jurisprudence—the Next Step* (1930) 30 COLUMBIA LAW REVIEW 431 and *Some Realism about Realism—Responding to Dean Pound* (1931) 44 HARVARD LAW REVIEW 1222; Patterson, *Pragmatism as a Philosophy of Law* in THE PHILOSOPHER OF THE COMMON MAN (1940) 172–204; Cohen, *Transcendental Nonsense and the Functional Approach* (1935) 35 COLUMBIA LAW REVIEW 809 and *Problems of Functional Jurisprudence* (1937) 1 MODERN LAW REVIEW 15; Frank, *Realism in Jurisprudence* (1934) 7 AMERICAN LAW SCHOOL REVIEW 1057. These are probably the best statements of this interest of realism. See the Selective Bibliography for others.

[2] The common center of contemporary American realistic jurisprudence is found in its critical temper and method. As in any movement, the emphasis of the realists is not entirely homogeneous, yet the variations are not of such a nature as to exclude a basic identity of interest. Llewellyn, *Some Realism about Realism* (1931) 44 HARVARD LAW REVIEW 1222, surveys the different emphases to be found among realists, together with their common basis. The common grounds which Llewellyn emphasizes are: (1) a common point of departure; and (2) a cross relevance, a complementing and interlocking of their varied results, and a common faith in their methods. The common points of departure which Llewellyn notes may be summarized as: (1) a conception of law in flux; (2) a conception of law as a means to social ends; (3) a conception of society in flux; (4) the temporary divorce of *is* and *ought* for purposes of study; (5) a distrust of traditional legal rules and concepts; (6) a distrust of the importance given to prescriptive rules in reaching decisions; (7) a belief in the value of grouping cases in narrower categories; (8) an insistence on evaluation in terms of effects; and (9) insistence on "programmatic and sustained attacks along these lines."

This is especially true in respect to the realists' primary interest in more adequate predictions and descriptions of what courts do in fact, an interest which is one phase of the larger interest in the criticism and reform of both the methods and the content of the existing system of law. The constant critical scrutiny of laws in respect of their descriptive adequacy has always been an essential part of the method of the good lawyer, whether as an advocate he prepared to argue cases or as a counselor he advised clients. As an advocate he must predict the effectiveness of legal arguments to evoke from the court the decision which he seeks; as a counselor he must predict the outcome of the course of action which he advises his client to take. Essentially, the realists have taken seriously the practical techniques of the lawyer and have transformed them into generalized and critical methods of research, thereby opening avenues of insight hitherto virtually untouched by an analytical and formal jurisprudence and affecting profoundly our settled convictions about law.[8]

The lawyer is interested in accurate knowledge of the operating factors that govern a given situation, on the basis of which he hopes to be better able to predict the outcome of specific future cases. What is significant in this procedure is that recourse to much more than the formulated statements in lawbooks is needed for this prediction. The attention of the lawyer is not infrequently directed to the question of whether a rule ought or ought not to be the rule for decision, but this attention is given because the correct answer will be one of the factors

[8] The realists have, many of them, turned their attention directly to a frank statement of the lawyer's procedure. See Isaacs, *How Lawyers Think* (1923) 23 COLUMBIA LAW REVIEW 555; Radin, *The Education of a Lawyer* (1937) 25 CALIFORNIA LAW REVIEW 676; Moore and Sussman, *The Lawyer's Law* (1932) 41 YALE LAW JOURNAL 566, 567. "An endeavor to understand the field of law must begin with the activities and ways of thinking of the practitioner."

which enables a prediction to be made respecting what will be the rule for a given decision. The extent to which rules of law do in fact describe what courts will actually do and the extent to which reliance may or may not be laced on stated doctrine are of primary interest. The meaning of a rule is determined by its effects upon the operations of judges or other officials.[4] Rules. then, for the lawyer are instruments; for him they are primarily instruments of prediction. Rules, if they are to be considered meaningful, must have an empirical relevance to actual procedures of courts.

The Austinian conception of law[5] as acts of command offers an insufficient theoretical and practical basis for all that the lawyer finds important in his work. The working formulae of the lawyer contain too much that is either ignored or unintelligible in the Austinian framework. Rules for the lawyer are comments in the sense of being shorthand expressions of much that is not understandable merely as acts of command or illustrations of sovereignty. A lawyer's interest in the problem of prediction is one which carries even a cursory investigation beyond the conventional legal formulae of statute, judicial opinion or treatise. The reason is that in predictions one is interested in the future actions of courts, and future actions, while indisputably grounded in a legal tradition, are equally rooted in present social practices and in what a critical evaluation of foreseen consequences implies for these present practices and the legal forms in which they are or will be crystallized.

In transforming the practicing lawyer's empirical procedures into a refined and thoroughgoing experimental approach and into a thoroughly functional and instru-

[4] See especially Frank, *What the Courts Do in Fact* (1932) 24 ILLINOIS LAW REVIEW 645 ff.

[5] AUSTIN, JURISPRUDENCE (4th ed.) I, 182.

mental conception of law, the American legal realists have in effect broken down a contradiction between the prevailing beliefs men had about law and the methods exemplified in the practice of law. For while the practice of law had its own implicit principles, reflective thinking about law had explicit formulations which took little account of these working principles. Men borrowed their thought about law not from the principles of practice but from traditional philosophies of law. These philosophies of law, with some exceptions as in the case of historical and sociological jurisprudence, operated with conceptions of the nature and method of law far removed from, if not irrelevant to, the *de facto* law with which the practicing lawyer and judge had an empirical acquaintance. Consequently, from the beginning the realists have directed their attention to a criticism of the prevailing philosophies of law and have made a concerted effort to meet the need for reconstructing our most general conceptions of law and its methods.[6]

This general interest in formulating more accurately the working principles of law was given significance, meaning, content, and direction by empirical, functional, and institutional investigations into specific bodies of

[6] See, for example, one of the earlier realists, Bingham, *What is the Law?* (1912) 11 MICHIGAN LAW REVIEW 1, 109. See also Hale, *Some Challenges to Conventional Legal Views* (1923) 9 AMERICAN BAR ASSOC. JOURNAL 330; Isaacs, *The Law and the Facts* (1922) 22 COLUMBIA LAW REVIEW 1. For the emphasis upon scientific method, see Yntema, *The Rational Basis of Legal Science* (1931) 31 COLUMBIA LAW REVIEW 925; Patterson, *Can Law Be Scientific?* (1930) 25 ILLINOIS LAW REVIEW 121; Llewellyn, *Legal Tradition and the Social Science Method* in ESSAYS ON RESEARCH IN THE SOCIAL SCIENCES (1931); Douglas and Thomas, *The Business Failure Project—a Study in Methodology* (1930) 39 YALE LAW JOURNAL 1013, (1931) 40 YALE LAW JOURNAL 1034; Oliphant, *Current Discussions of Legal Methodology* (1921) 7 AMERICAN BAR ASSOC. JOURNAL 241, Radin, *Scientific Method and the Law* (1931) 19 CALIFORNIA LAW REVIEW 164; Cook, *Scientific Method and the Law* (1927) 13 AMERICAN BAR ASSOC JOURNAL 303 See the bibliography of realism, "Realistic Jurisprudence," at the end and note the many studies concerned with this problem of an empirical methodology.

law, specific court practices, and into the specific interrelations of laws and social practices. Today there are few branches of law where the influence of an instrumentalist approach has not been felt. In every direction, the attempt to understand laws in terms of what they do and in terms of how they operate is altering the actual structures and operations of law, as well as our understanding of that law.[7] Whether the field be that of torts, procedure, contracts, legislation, constitutional law, business, or administrative law, the results of such activity are apparent. The general effect of these studies has been to clarify the need for, and the importance of, fundamental revisions of the concepts of law, and even where revision is not imperative, there is yet a different conception of the specific role of concepts. Only a few of the larger concepts which have received attention need to be mentioned: in the law of contract, the idea of contract itself, the conventional analysis into offer and acceptance, the doctrine of consideration, the theory of reasonable expectation, and the relation of contract to quasi contract; in tort law, the doctrines of reasonableness, proximate cause, and negligence; in the law of property, the idea of property[8] and the doctrine of nuisance; in criminal law, the conceptions of accessory, malice, *mens rea,* and attempt; in constitutional law, the conceptions of due process, states' rights, freedom of contract, and delegation of powers. The number of studies of more particularized concepts is legion.

REALISTIC NEGATIONS

Throughout these various investigations and especially in the various initial efforts to formulate the theoretical

[7] For an earlier selective bibliography of actual work done on law by realists, see Llewellyn, *Some Realism about Realism* (1931) 44 HARVARD LAW REVIEW 1222.

[8] Especially the connection of property with tax power and such questions as who "owned" what within a corporate structure.

foundations of realism, the burden of criticism was negative in its emphasis, consisting for the most part of destructive criticism of prevailing concepts and vigorous denunciations of previous theories about or formulations of law that had emphasized the formal and systematic organization of the existing principles. Furthermore, the realists found that an empirical approach to law led to emphasis on the relationships existing between law and its content on the one hand and such other disciplines as anthropology, psychology, economics, and sociology and their respective subject matters on the other and to a study of the operation of what courts do in these various contests.[9] This combined emphasis on the need to understand law in terms of all that enters into and affects its operation and the critical attitude that realists assume toward an excessive logical emphasis have had the general effect of convincing many that legal realism takes an irrational approach to law, denying to law any significant logical or systematic character.

What realism has attacked is, however, not logic but the tendency to use logic alone with insufficient concern

[9] For the economic emphasis, see HALE, LEGAL FACTORS IN ECONOMIC SOCIETY (1937) and *Force and the State: a Comparison of "Political" and "Economic" Compulsion* (1935) 35 COLUMBIA LAW REVIEW 149; HALL, THEFT, LAW AND SOCIETY (1935); Llewellyn, *Through Title to Contract and a Bit Beyond* (1938) 15 NEW YORK UNIVERSITY LAW QUARTERLY REVIEW 159; Pickett, *Nicknames and Unfair Competition* (1935) 35 COLUMBIA LAW REVIEW 33.

For the sociological emphasis, see Moore, *The Rational Basis of Legal Institutions* (1923) 23 COLUMBIA LAW REVIEW 609 and *An Institutional Approach to the Law of Commercial Banking* (1928) 38 YALE LAW JOURNAL 703; Frank, *Institutional Analysis of Law* (1924) 24 COLUMBIA LAW REVIEW 480; Moore, Sussman, and Corstvet, *Drawing against Uncollected Checks* (1935) 45 YALE LAW JOURNAL 1, 260; CAIRNES, LAW AND THE SOCIAL SCIENCES (1935) and *Law and Anthropology* (1931) 31 COLUMBIA LAW REVIEW 32; Llewellyn, *On Warranty of Quality* (1936) 36 COLUMBIA LAW REVIEW 699, (1937) 37 COLUMBIA LAW REVIEW 341.

For the psychological emphasis, see ROBINSON, LAW AND THE LAWYERS (1935), especially Chapters IV–VIII; FRANK, LAW AND THE MODERN MIND (1930); Cook, *Act Intention and Motive in the Criminal Law* (1916) 26 YALE LAW JOURNAL 645; BURTT, LEGAL PSYCHOLOGY (1931).

for any but the formal character of the premises.[10] Its own aim is an adequate, though thus far unobtainable, logical structure. It attacks not consistency but inadequately based rationalization, not the syllogism but the misdirected use of the syllogism and the content of particular syllogisms. It is critical of the power of logic exclusively to control law: first, because logic has been, and probably will be, unable to do so; and, second, because to improve law more than logic is necessary unless logic operates from premises-to-be-formed as readily as from premises-in-stock. Descriptively, it denies that logic in fact controls law. Even as an ideal, the value of logical form is limited in that techniques require a flexibility to adapt law to new interests, especially in a dynamic culture. Realism demands not less logic but more intelligence in regard to the methods and premises involved in the use of logic. The tendency to use a deductive logic mechanically and the tendency to use ancient formulae exclusively as premises are the greatest obstacles which realism finds to better understanding and effective control of law.[11] Basically, the realistic criticisms are not of concepts but of what happens to concepts when they are uncritically used and when their role as instruments is insufficiently emphasized. A most casual survey of realistic legal studies would indicate that the realists' objective is not

[10] The best illustrations of this are in Llewellyn, *The Rule of Law in Our Case Law of Contract* (1938) 47 YALE LAW JOURNAL 1243 and *Our Case Law of Contract: Offer and Acceptance* (1938) 48 YALE LAW JOURNAL 1, 9 ff.

[11] For a strong statement of this, see Nelles, *Toward Legal Understanding* (1934) 34 COLUMBIA LAW REVIEW 862, 1041. On the other hand, that the realist is interested in logical analysis and symmetry is clearly evident in realists like Corbin and Goble. See, for example, Goble, *A Redefinition of Basic Legal Terms* (1935) 35 COLUMBIA LAW REVIEW 535 and *Negative Legal Relations Reexamined* (1922) 6 ILLINOIS LAW REVIEW 36; Corbin, *Rights and Duties* (1924) 33 YALE LAW JOURNAL 501 and *Legal Analysis and Terminology* (1919) 29 YALE LAW JOURNAL 163.

the elimination of concepts but, on the contrary, an emphasis upon the multiplication of concepts and working categories.[12] But the emphasis includes a realization that rules are instruments as well as ends of judgments and that as instruments and as ends they have a social relevance and dimension to which they are initially sensitive and to which they must be kept sensitive. Nor have the realists reduced law to something else—to economics, to psychology, or to physics. The realists have asserted, however, that law is not something isolated and separate from society; for them law is completely understood only as the ways of law are seen as part of the very fabric of social ways.[13]

Unfortunately, the fruitful results attained by the realists have been somewhat obscured. The realists, in recognizing the underlying bias of the characteristic traditional emphasis in law, often overreached in seeking arguments and illustrations which would bring into the sharpest focus possible the weakness of the more usual approach. Not always content with a factual and operational approach to their own problems, nor satisfied with providing evidence of the irrelevance of most of the prevailing philosophies to the pressing needs of law, and proceeding cautiously to state the realists' own method and perspective, some realists brought confusion into their arguments by attitudes and analyses which are misleading if not erroneous. This has brought about the opposition and misunderstanding of such men as Morris R. Cohen, Kantorowicz, Kocourek, Pound, Dickinson, and

[12] For a forceful statement of this, see Oliphant, *The Return to Stare Decisis* (1928) 14 AMERICAN BAR ASSOC. JOURNAL 70. He puts the issue as a shift from *stare dicta* to *stare decisis*.

[13] ROBINSON, LAW AND THE LAWYERS (1935) 327: "Obviously law is not identical with economics, sociology or psychology, but insistence on its *over-and-aboveness* has tended to insulate it from those very facts needed in the design of effective social control."

others.[14] The criticisms of these men were, in part at least, justified by the positions taken by some of the extreme realists. Thus, J. W. Bingham, one of the first and most extreme of the realists, weakened an otherwise incisive argument by resorting to an extreme nominalism which was quite unnecessary to the argument and made unrealistic assumptions as to the nature of rules and of generalizations.[15] Jerome Frank rested much of his analysis upon psychoanalytic interpretations of the traditional

[14] Cohen, *A Critical Review of the Last Hundred Years of American Jurisprudence* in LAW, A CENTURY OF PROGRESS, 1835–1935 (1937) II, 266; Kantorowicz, *Some Rationalism about Realism* (1934) 43 YALE LAW JOURNAL 1240; Kocourek (a criticism of Bingham), (1913) 9 ILLINOIS LAW REVIEW 138; Pound, *The Call for a Realistic Jurisprudence* (1931) 44 HARVARD LAW REVIEW 697; Dickinson, *Legal Rules and the Process of Decision* (1931) 79 UNIVERSITY OF PENNSYLVANIA LAW REVIEW 833 and *Legal Rules: Their Application and Elaboration* (1931) 79 UNIVERSITY OF PENNSYLVANIA LAW REVIEW 1052. Dickinson's criticisms of the realists' conception of rules, like most of the others, rested upon a misunderstanding; the realists for their part have heartily accepted his own fine analysis of rules and principles. Fuller, *American Legal Realism* (1934) 82 UNIVERSITY OF PENNSYLVANIA LAW REVIEW 429, makes a fair evaluation of realism except that he wrongly insists that the realist is overemphasizing the rightness of the actual. Kennedy has been the most persistent critic of legal realism. See, for example, his *Realism, What Next?* (1938) 7 FORDHAM LAW REVIEW 203. See the bibliography, "Criticism and Evaluation of Legal Realism," at the end for a list of his articles criticizing realism. The fairest criticism is probably by Cardozo, who at the time of writing was not sure whether he was a realist or not. His sympathy, however, permitted him to go to the heart of realism and to avoid the obvious misunderstandings. See his address printed in (1932) 55 NEW YORK BAR ASSOCIATION REPORTS 263. For other critical estimates of realism, see the Selective Bibliography.

[15] Bingham, *What is the Law?* (1912) 11 MICHIGAN LAW REVIEW 1; this was followed by *Science and the Law* (1913) 25 GREEN BAG 162, by *Legal Philosophy and the Law* (1914) 9 ILLINOIS LAW REVIEW 98, and by *The Nature and Importance of Legal Possession* (1915) 13 MICHIGAN LAW REVIEW 535. "Rules are not outside the mind and are not discovered; they are psychological. Ideas are not copies of the world; language is not a copy of either." There are no "first" realists in law, but Bingham came close to achieving the title by virtue of the very vigor of his writing. It should be noted that Bingham recognized the necessary role of generalizations in law. "The intelligent direction of human action," writes Bingham in 11 MICHIGAN LAW REVIEW 35, "necessarily involves the use of generalizations. Generalizations therefore have a causative force in producing legal effects . . . but they are not the whole field."

emphasis on the ideal of certainty and logical form, which even he later recognized to be built of straw.[16] Thurman Arnold criticized theories in law in terms of a series of incisive caricatures which, if taken strictly, appear to necessitate the view that all reflective analyses and ideal projections are but the rantings of lunatics.[17]

The effect of such writing has been to play into the hands of those who feel that an understanding of law is better realized through other means and by a more conservative approach. Nevertheless, the results of a realistic approach to the problem of describing existing laws far outweigh the excesses its more enthusiastic adherents may have committed. As a program of action and as a method of analysis, it remains inescapably fixed as an extremely important and fruitful contribution to the better appreciation of the present content of law, the full effects of which method we have yet to see.

REALISM AND JUSTICE

If the emphasis of American legal realism upon the interrelations of law and life and upon empirical methods of investigation has been fruitful of better predictability, this emphasis has as well a special relevance to problems of justice. The concern of realism with laws as predictions, with the methods, techniques, assumptions, content, and meaning of existing laws, leads to a concern for both the general theory and the particular problems of justice. It leads to these problems in the sense that they are implied in a consideration of laws which are viewed as predictions and in the sense that these problems are the contexts which make prediction itself a moral concern. It leads to a reconsideration of the gen-

[16] FRANK, LAW AND THE MODERN MIND (1930); see Appendix X to the 1931 reprint and his reference to the book in SAVE AMERICA FIRST (1938).

[17] Arnold is discussed below, pp. 15–17, 108–13.

eral theory of justice, because the introduction of empirical methods in law affects seriously many of the reigning assumptions of existing theories—assumptions which are not compatible with empirical methods as applied to problems of justice.

One who reads the literature of American legal realism will discover many indications of the presence of an altered conception of the character of the quest for justice. The literature exhibits a more empirical, pragmatic emphasis in the approach to normative problems than has hitherto been generally found in practice or given due recognition in theory. Yet an empirical approach to the problems of justice has appeared to many to be insidious if not, in fact, a rejection of all concern for justice.[18] It has been interpreted as a denial of the possibility of serious consideration of what ought to be, a substitution of the individual prejudice in the judge for impartial judgment in accordance with principle, or as a complacency with the actual as it is. W. B. Kennedy writes: "There is grave danger that functionalism [legal realism] having turned to the study of facts, things, and tangibles may end by shutting itself up in that reality and closing the mind to the consideration, analysis, and evaluation of the facts."[19] A functional or empirical approach, it is argued, is to take the short range view, to make standards either impossible, irrelevant, or a matter primarily of subjective selection.[20]

Here again, as in the related problem discussed above, the realists themselves have not been free either from this feeling or from the responsibility of having created

[18] See also Stone, *Pound's Theory of Justice, a Critique* (1935) 20 Iowa Law Review 531.

[19] *Functional Nonsense and the Transcendental Approach* (1936) 5 Fordham Law Review 272, 276. See Hutchins, *Autobiography of an Ex-Law Student* (1934) 7 American Law School Review 1051.

[20] Kennedy, *Pragmatism as a Philosophy of Law* (1924) 9 Marquette Law Review 63 and *Men or Laws* (1932) 2 Brooklyn Law Review 11.

this impression in others. This is abundantly illustrated in the writings of Thurman W. Arnold. Both in *The Symbols of Government* and *The Folklore of Capitalism* Arnold presents a thesis which has for its purpose the reconstruction of our attitudes toward law, its institutions, and its methods. Proposing to look at law objectively, he urges that to the trained eye of a politician theory is rationalization and functions primarily as an emotional symbol to clothe action. Theories of government are symbols of government; they are projected verbal ideals, dramatizations of what individuals and institutions prefer to picture themselves as either being or seeking, removed from any intelligent reference to what they are or what they are achieving.[21] Theories of social institutions are important as decorative aspects of life. "Yet important as they are in their place they are not the tools by which discoveries are made."[22] The difficulty here is that Arnold appears to make necessary the consignment of his own book about symbols to the class of folklore, and with it goes the whole theoretical underpinning of realistic evaluation and reform. If any and every farsighted approach to the observation and reform of the institutions of society makes a man a priest and so only of importance as a producer of merely emotive symbols, then Arnold logically condemns all evaluation and all attempts to make action intelligent. The difference between a priest and a scientist is not, however, the difference between an approach and no approach; rather it is the difference between one method and another. Arnold's language draws a false and almost vicious dichotomy between having and

[21] Arnold, *Theories about Economic Theories* (1934) 26 ANNALS OF AMERICAN ACADEMY OF POLITICAL AND SOCIAL SCIENCE. See also his *Trial by Combat and the New Deal* (1933) 47 HARVARD LAW REVIEW 913 and *Criminal Attempts—the Rise and Fall of an Abstraction* (1930) 40 YALE LAW JOURNAL 53.

[22] THE SYMBOLS OF GOVERNMENT (1935) iv.

projecting ideals (called studying ritual "in the light of faiths and symbols") and scientific observation. The consequence of this is to make men foolish and scientific method unenlightened. Arnold, as a spokesman of this group, sees legal realism as rejecting ideals except as a necessary protective coloration for the actual business of getting things done. Such a view could be expected from one who is thoroughly at odds with contemporary legal realism, but it is disturbing to hear this from a realist. So to state the situation is to take the opponents' estimate of realism.

The disparity between what realists are doing and the impression they give of what they are doing is unfortunate, particularly as it relates to their conceptions of the purposes of law and the nature of legal evaluation.[23] Fully recognizing the changed conception of law involved in an empirical approach, legal realists have not sufficiently recognized that this implies a significant change in the manner of looking at values and valuation in law.[24] No realist would accept an unrealistic definition of law, but there has been a tendency to accept an equally foreign conception of evaluation and purposive activity. Of course, in accepting the opinions of others as to the nature of purposive action, realists subsequently find such a conception to be irrelevant. This has interesting consequences. When, for example, Arnold does, in fact, refer to standards, we have a shy reference to "benevolence,"

[23] Max Lerner's estimate expresses well the reaction of the reader to Arnold's writings. It gives the impression that "the social good which it [society] has failed to achieve by rational effort can be won by being fragmentized and pursued with desperate immediacy." *The Shadow World of Thurman Arnold* (1938) 47 YALE LAW JOURNAL 687, 694.

[24] See, for example, Beutel, *Some Implications of Experimental Jurisprudence* (1934) 48 HARVARD LAW REVIEW 169, 179: "The ethical problem of what is the highest good is today too far away to require consideration." Beutel reverses the usual emphasis: before talking about the good, one must first develop a full experimental technique. This position is, however, modified considerably toward the end of the article.

"humanitarianism," and "the respectable citizens," each of which falls in the line of fire of his previous criticism. When Hook[25] pointed this out, Arnold[26] replied that he eschews evaluation or reference to ethical standards, because this procedure involves first defining the good life and then trying to see how far human institutions have deviated from this subjective notion of the good life. Yet Arnold's own work is a testimony to a different conception.[27] It is clear that Arnold's interest has been to describe, sometimes with superb humor, the activities of government and the use men make of language and ideas. He is not to be held responsible for framing a theory of ends when such is not his purpose. It is true that his description of society has a moral interest, but this does not imply the necessity of clearly formulating what it means to have an interest in improvement. In general, the practical interests of the legal realists do not require that the conception of justice which they assume be fully formulated. But the conceptions assumed do not, therefore, become vain when made explicit.

"Normation"[28] in general and reflection on the purposes of law in particular are not matters which pass with the passing of a "conceptual" jurisprudence. Legal realism has done much to affect our thinking about the just judgment, and its implicit conception of the just judg-

[25] In a review of THE FOLKLORE OF CAPITALISM in (1938) 5 UNIVERSITY OF CHICAGO LAW REVIEW 341 and *Neither Myth nor Power—a Rejoinder* (1939) 5 UNIVERSITY OF CHICAGO LAW REVIEW 356.

[26] *The Folklore of Mr. Hook—a Reply* (1938) 5 UNIVERSITY OF CHICAGO LAW REVIEW 349, 354.

[27] See an illuminating article in this connection, Levi, *Natural Law, Precedent, and Thurman Arnold* (1938) 24 VIRGINIA LAW REVIEW 586. Levi clearly focuses attention upon the essential continuity of contemporary legal realism with the implicit objectives of "natural law" in its ameliorative phases.

[28] This word, coined by Llewellyn, is a convenient term to indicate the empirical fact that men discover and construct standards and make effective those which are given.

ment deserves an explicit statement. So fundamental is the conception of justice to the legal realist and so thoroughly is prescription, for legal realism, a basic context of prediction when the method and consequences of prediction are generalized, that to make explicit a realistic and functional view of justice is imperative. Of course, judgment of the realists' worth will rest by their own criterion upon their power to get things done that need getting done. The adequacy of their approach and their method will be decided not by abstract discussions of their operating assumptions but by the concrete results of the realistic approach; their use, by the value of their specific recommendations. Only a small group of realists, such as K. N. Llewellyn, F. Frankfurter, W. W. Cook, F. S. Cohen, M. Radin, E. Patterson, and a few others, are interested in the more general questions which these activities of research suggest. Nevertheless, an interested observer is led to inquire especially of these many specific studies not merely what the recommendations are but what in realistic terms are recommendations and what are the postulates and assumptions that make them intelligible. What justice is, as it reveals itself in the judicial process, when that process is interpreted as the American legal realist has interpreted it, brings to light enduring features which often have become apparent to reflective thinkers, but such an approach to justice places special emphasis on some phases of the conception which frequently have been neglected. A consideration of some of the features and emphases that go to make up a realistic view of justice will be made in the following chapters.

A statement of a theory of justice which bases itself on work which has been primarily concerned with the judicial process will inevitably reflect that central focus. The focal interest here, then, will be the judge's justice, the features of justice that become important within the judicial process, and the subject matter will, therefore, be limited in scope. What the problems or principles of justice are with respect to the community of all living things comprises possibly distinct but not wholly separable features with which, at any rate, this book is not immediately concerned. It is the implications of the contemporary American realistic approach to law for the theory of the just judgment within the sphere of the court that these chapters will seek to clarify.

CHAPTER II

THE PROBLEMATIC IN JUSTICE

THE SEARCH for justice is the major enterprise of law, and the attempt to characterize justice is inseparably connected with that which characterizes law. Justice not only gives rise to law but arises out of law. It is the cause of law in the same way that any basic need is the cause of the practical art which seeks to meet that need. Justice is also the consequence of law in the same way that any instrument suggests and transforms its ends.[1] K. N. Llewellyn has characterized law as the "repair shop" of society; but a repair shop, centering its attention on imperfections, may be the most fruitful source of insight into actual and possible perfections, giving the impetus to "put in running order" the object it repairs.

THE CONTEXT OF JUSTICE

Law as an ongoing process has its focus in the activities of judgment.[2] The problems of law are problems of judgment, and judgment is the activity of making deci-

[1] See HOOK, THE METAPHYSICS OF PRAGMATISM (1927) 58: "Instead of forging instruments to initiate changes for the sake of an ultimate good which does not itself change, instruments are often wiser and more potent than those who made them, and shift the ultimate reference farther and farther from the specific terminus that called them into being."

[2] Llewellyn, *Legal Tradition and Social Science Method* in ESSAYS ON RESEARCH IN THE SOCIAL SCIENCES (1931) 91: "Disputes are the eternal heart and core of the law. They do not mark its circumference, but they will always mark its center."

sions. In this sense, law is evaluation. Yet, law is also evaluated, for the evaluations which judgment both uses and makes are neither self-evidently correct nor independent of other estimation and criticism. Such evaluations of judgment, as well as the criticism of procedures, while engaged in by many agencies in a community, have their foci in the constant self-criticism that the law makes of its own products and instruments. In fact, the crucial criticism of law is so intertwined with the legal judgment itself that the process is essentially one, and to draw a distinction between judgments *by* law and *of* law requires a surgical operation upon a unified process. In focusing standards and ends upon particular problems, law brings the most vital critique possible to bear upon the adequacy of its standards and ideals.[3] Upon this fact depends the vitality of the legal process and the estimation of the worth of different judges and judgments.

Not all law is just nor is justice law. The distinction between the two cuts many ways. Law may be either just or unjust; both judges and laws miss the mark, become petrified, and fail to meet needs. But law and justice cannot be intelligibly separated into radically different categories. They are distinctions within a common process, and neither can be entirely understood apart from the other. Law itself, apart from justice, is a blind mechanism and dangerously lunatic; justice, apart from its potential embodiment in law, is idle fancy. Not every judgment is just, but justice must be a possible judgment. What law ought to be is what justice is, but what justice can be depends upon, and is limited by, what legal judgment is.[4] Justice may properly be said to be the ideal of

[3] See Cohen, *The Ethical Basis of Legal Criticism* (1931) 41 YALE LAW JOURNAL 201. See also his ETHICAL SYSTEMS AND LEGAL IDEALS (1933) Part I.

[4] Cohen, *The Problems of Functional Jurisprudence* (1937) 1 MODERN LAW REVIEW 15, emphasizes heavily the realist's interest in empirical de-

judgment, but "ideal" justice is not the most significant phase of justice. To initiate an inquiry by turning to ideal justice is to risk distorting both law and justice. Such a procedure is likely to make justice unreal and reality unillumined. We turn then to the empirical character and content of justice as revealed in law taken as a process of judgment.

What meets the inquirer in considering the subject matter and the content of judgment in the legal process is the endless multiplicity of the contexts of judgments and evaluation. Locating the planes of reference for the significance of a dispute is at the very heart of judgment. Sometimes the context of a decision is relatively singular, yet frequently a dispute requires settlement in the light of far reaching, universal, complex, and, oftentimes, vaguely defined contexts. Such is frequently the situation when judgment is reached by means of direct reference to "justice." When this is done, we may expect to hear strong words of protest from sincere nominalists, positivists, and debunkers. Yet even where justice and the principles of law are, in fact, used without determinate meaning, even where they are deliberately employed because of their vagueness to manipulate situations, there may be neither legal malfeasance, negligence, nor stupidity involved. Only too frequently for a neat, systematic analysis of law, situations are met where stresses operate in terms of contexts with limits which are themselves problematic.[5] Ultimately the whole context of interests may be involved in a single judgment.

The use of wide contexts is criticized by some because under the cloak of generality are hidden the private interests of individuals. Yet materialistic criticism estab-

---

terminations for particular conflicts of the limits, powers, and defects of legal judgments.

[5] *Ibid.*, 10.

lished no new principle when it asserted that much of any legal doctrine operates as a moral screen to hide the nakedness and rawness of private interests. That interests are ultimately private and values ultimately interests is recognized by any empirical view. Yet it would be indeed a strange empiricism that did not recognize at the same time the *de facto* existence of meaningful reference to patterns, totalities, complexes, and organic interrelations in experience. Reference to, and the use of, constitutional limitations in an attack upon a law which restrains the employer from interfering with the organization of his employees into an effective bargaining unit operates as a defense of the private profit of the individual, but it is no less a meaningful reference to a significant context. The "tyranny of words" is possible only because symbols are also keys to doors which open to the light. Were they not instruments of vision, they would have little power as instruments of darkness.[6]

THE REALM OF PRECEDENT

Reference in legal argument to larger contexts, wider planes of interpretation than that of the immediately "given"—which is really the "narrowly taken"—is not only possible but inevitable. Were this not the case, we might witness a truly atomic science of law, which law, if the idea is itself not contradictory, would be to renounce all attempts at generalization in analysis.[7] In the operation

[6] The characteristics of the contexts to which we refer are subject to criticism. Whether the contexts are to be entirely of the market place and of action or of some other character depends in part upon our special interests. The criticism of legal contexts has in recent years been most emphasized by the realists. See p. 7, note 6.

[7] The reason for emphasizing this is to avoid what for the most part is irrelevant criticism of realistic jurisprudence, namely, that it attempts to reduce all subject matter to pure particularity. See Patterson, *The Restatement of the Law of Contracts* (1933) 33 COLUMBIA LAW REVIEW 397, 423 ff., which presents well the relative difference between legal realism and the type of approach to law which produced the restatement as its fulfillment.

of the English and American institutions of law, the notion of precedent commonly serves to define contexts and may, therefore, be used as an illustration. The idea of precedent with its constituent factors, such as *stare decisis, ratio decidendi*, and *obiter dicta*, is a simple and at the same time apposite example of the fact of reference. The principle of judicial decision that there must be in general a precedent for any particular decision is a distinct recognition of the importance of contexts, of the fact that no conflict is autonomous, related only numerically, formally, or by accident to the rest of the events and patterns of events in the communities in which we live. This principle converts, as is so frequently done, a relative necessity and a useful instrument into a duty. The Anglo-American insistence upon a particular precedent implies more than a peculiar penchant for the concrete universal, but it signifies that at least.[8] Basically what is sought in precedent, what is relied upon in the reference to precedent, is not the individual decision as such but some universal exemplified in some adjudicated situation.[9] An attempt to make the *ratio decidendi* a species of *obiter dicta* and to make of this *obiter dicta* merely a form of "secular prayer" or a ritual,[10] if taken seriously, would lead to an atomic law. But the fact that one case makes a precedent only under peculiar and fairly specifiable conditions, that what makes a significant precedent is the series and the pattern of cases, should make

[8] See Oliphant, *The Return to Stare Decisis* (1928) 14 AMERICAN BAR ASSOC. JOURNAL 159.

[9] The value of the "case method" of instruction in the law school depends upon the emphasis it places upon training the student to elicit from the case workable rules or universals. See Radin, *The Education of a Lawyer* (1937) 25 CALIFORNIA LAW REVIEW 676. It is not, as Radin points out, merely another way of presenting the "correct" rule.

[10] See some of Frank's statements in LAW AND THE MODERN MIND, Chapter XIV. It should be said in defense of Frank that despite the generality of his statements he has in mind the trial court primarily.

us cautious of any attempt so to nominalize our conception of law.

That precedent is used to give clues to contexts, indicia of the meanings of the present conflict, or in general gives material which assists in the formulation of the subject matter at hand is attested to by anyone familiar at all with the operation of American or English law. It is this character of the idea of precedent which is at the heart of its value in our Western tradition. But the reference to precedent is no touchstone. Its primary significance lies in the fact that it illustrates and illumines multiple and possible contexts in so far as the working mechanism of the law has discovered, invented, or utilized them.[11] "If holdings are to be read, not as general rules, but in the light of their particulars, the past may be invoked as experience rather than as compulsion."[12] The circumstances which make necessary the reference to precedent are at the same time the circumstances that make half impotent the appeal to precedent. Conflicts come before courts, and the bickering of lawyers makes known the fact that there is a conflict. But what that conflict is is not self-evident. We have rules of procedure and categories of causes which operate as pigeonholes for the allocation of the more immediate and familiar facts. When law was primarily an affair of writs, the responsibility for properly defining and locating the significant issues rested almost exclusively on the individual, courts utilizing for the most part the techniques applicable to the form in which the conflict was presented.[13] Today

[11] Llewellyn has presented this phase of the doctrine of *stare decisis* in his PRÄJUDIZIENRECHT UND RECHTSPRECHUNG IN AMERIKA (1933) Part I. See also Patterson, *Can Law be Scientific?* (1930) 25 ILLINOIS LAW REVIEW 121, 135 ff.

[12] Hamilton, *Preview of a Justice* (1939) 48 YALE LAW JOURNAL 819, 823.

[13] Maitland, *The History of the Register of Original Writs* (1888) 3 HARVARD LAW REVIEW 212; cited by Oliphant, *The Return to Stare Decisis* (1928) 14 AMERICAN BAR ASSOC. JOURNAL 13.

the pleading and definition of causes is roughly a co-operative enterprise between lawyer and court; the lawyer offers a preliminary analysis of what the meaning of the conflict is, but the ultimate responsibility rests with the court to establish that meaning authoritatively. The conflict is precisely what it is and nothing else, but the conflict cannot be treated intelligibly and with reason unless that conflict is analyzable into its important elements and is seen in its past and probable contexts as defined usually by the aid of precedent.

Oliphant[14] analyzes a simple situation which illustrates the ingrained character of plurality of contexts and considerations in the lawyer's treatment of the problematic.[15] His example is that of a suit brought by a fiancé against the father of the girl who was to be the bride; the plaintiff alleges that the father induced his daughter to break her promise to marry the plaintiff; relief is sought in damages. Strictly speaking, the conflict involves individuals *A, B,* and *C* in all their particularity; it involves the special history of this case; it involves everything in short which gives the situation its "thisness." As an event it has few precise limits. Everything in the past, up to the time of trial, is potentially material. The relevant facts for the decision of that case must be in part constructed in the course of litigation and decision. Our own social habits of speech, our usual classifications, immediately enable us to speak not only of John, Jane, and Joe, but of father, daughter, and fiancé. Statements made by the father are found, or alleged, to be words inducing breach of promise. But the court in defining the problem could with legitimacy have as the facts of the conflict John, Jane, and Joe; boy, father, and girl; or men and women.

[14] *The Return to Stare Decisis* (1928) 14 AMERICAN BAR ASSOC. JOURNAL 71, 159.

[15] One of the most vigorous statements of this important phase of the law is also given by Frank, *What Courts Do in Fact* (1932) 24 ILLINOIS LAW REVIEW 645, 653 ff.

The statements made could be considered as merely statements of advice, command, suggestion, discussion or, on the other hand, as words inducing a breach of promise to marry, thence as words inducing a breach of any promise, and thence as any conduct inducing a breach of any promise. The judge chooses at his peril and at the peril of the situation any of these contexts. The range of legal consequences of using each may be entirely different and usually is; for the meanings and relations each make pertinent vary widely. And yet they are all contexts and considerations of this conflict.

Felix Cohen's "Transcendental Nonsense and the Functional Approach"[16] treats critically another illustration of the problematic context. Here, as contrasted with the preceding, the problem is slightly altered. For, whereas the suit of the fiancé involved the definition of the relevant universal, Cohen's discussion[17] is centered around the definition and proper selection of a complete perspective of universals, or in Oliphant's language, the proper "pyramid"[18] of which the case should serve as the apex and in which different levels of interpretation were equally present as universals.[19] The particular case in question concerned a corporation created in Pennsylvania but doing business in New York.[20] The corporation was sued in New York; it objected to the suit on the

[16] (1935) 35 Columbia Law Review 809.

[17] *Ibid.*, 810.

[18] *The Return to Stare Decisis* (1928) American Bar Assoc. Journal 159.

[19] An illustration of this is to be found in the manner in which courts altered and shifted their categories in their treatment of a joint deposit in a bank while the right of survivorship was involved, a so-called poor man's will. Some courts called it a trust—122 Cal. 19 (1898)—a contract—126 Me. 84 (1927)—a contract creating a joint tenancy—82 W. Va. 9 (1918)—a joint tenancy—310 Ill. 185 (1923)—a gift—195 Mich. 502 (1914)—a third party beneficiary contract—120 Va. 297 (1917)—an agency—110 Me. 32 (1912)—or a testamentary disposition—120 Va. 297 (1917). This aspect of the law governing the facts is discussed in (1928) 24 Virginia Law Review 586.

[20] Tauza v. Susquehanna Coal Co., 220 N.Y. 259, 115 N.E. 915 (1917).

ground that it was not a resident of the state in which the suit was brought. The question raised, or the definition of the issue as it was stated by the court, was phrased in terms of locating the corporation, in the same manner as one might seek to find the legal residence of an individual.

Cohen writes:

> On the basis of facts revealed by an inquiry [into the practices of corporations, difficulties, etc.] and on the basis of certain political or ethical value judgments as to the propriety of putting financial burdens upon corporations a competent legislature would have attempted to formulate some rule as to when a foreign corporation should be subject to suit.[21]

But such considerations were passed by, so far as the explicit record of the case is concerned, and the problem was treated in terms of the "fictitious" question of the locus of a corporation. Kennedy criticizes this analysis, for while Cohen equates this problem with the problem of "angels on a needlepoint," he, nevertheless, continues to treat the idea of a corporation as meaningful and the problems of locus and of jurisdictional limitation as significant.[22] No such easy criticism is adequate once it is understood that Cohen is not criticizing the use of these ideas but is criticizing the mismanagement of a particular case and the frequent tendency of courts to select for the focus of attention those problems which often have the least possible reference to social situations which generate the issues. Admittedly, the question of the jurisdiction of the court is a legitimate possible question to raise and in some cases it is the important question. Whether or not this specific case rightfully raised the issue is subject to debate. We are not immediately concerned with

[21] (1935) 35 COLUMBIA LAW REVIEW 814.

[22] Kennedy, *Functional Nonsense and the Transcendental Approach* (1936) 5 FORDHAM LAW REVIEW 272, 290.

this issue, except to note that the determination of what the conflict was is subject to debate precisely because the facts say nothing determinately. They offer divergent possibilities.[23] The possible categories for the illumination of the situation are not all of equal value: the choice of one leads to one conclusion of the dispute; the choice of another leads to entirely different results. The initial problem is thus the problem of defining or circumscribing the problem. For its definition, the courts rely upon, and are controlled mostly by, precedent.[24] But neither precedent nor the conflict itself gives a ready-made answer. For the quest for the definition of the issues themselves is never entirely impartial. The definition by the court of the meaning of a conflict depends in part upon the consequences implied by that meaning. Here, as elsewhere, the instrument is potentially a "device." The choice of what is the conflict is correlatively dependent on a hypothesis of what is to be done, the two hang together and are never entirely separable. Down to the policeman on his beat, categories are chosen as well as followed.[25] What is cannot be separated from what is wanted, because what is, for human purposes, is what it is said to be and what anything is said to be depends in part upon what consequences are wanted to follow. In other words, what a case is said to have been is deter-

[23] Such divergent possibilities actually operate on the same state of facts. See Llewellyn, *Across Sales on Horseback* (1939) 52 HARVARD LAW REVIEW 725. The question of ownership in the field of sales is illustrative (*Ibid.*, 733): "The wares may be 'sellers' for proper stoppage in transit, and yet be 'his buyers' for purposes of action on the price, and yet again be 'eithers' for purposes of recovering damage suffered in transit—and all on the same facts."

[24] "Precedent" has a general use—to suggest categories for isolating and defining an issue—and a special use—to indicate particular rules applicable to an issue as defined. Neither use is entirely separable from a given situation. We are interested here in its use as a clarifier of issues.

[25] One of the most important functions of categories is their systematic misuse; for a discussion of the use of alternative precedents see Corwin, *The Schechter Case* in LAW, A CENTURY OF PROGRESS (1937) II, 32.

mined in part by what we hope it may "turn out" to be. Yet, the quest for what is is never entirely arbitrary or artificial. The problematic character is real and peculiarly alive in those events which have legal significance. Precedent as a record of past analysis serves to suggest what may again be, but whatever concept is chosen either by way of analogy or of clear precedent is always in strictness hypothetical and relative to changing conditions.

The teleological or functional character of categories is well illustrated in the concept of jurisdiction. The question arises as to what is the jurisdiction of a particular court; the answer will vary as the purposes for which jurisdiction is sought vary. Thus jurisdiction may be different for cases which involve such problems as procedural, criminal, or tax issues. The jurisdiction may also vary within any of these. Jurisdiction for purposes of taxation, for example, will depend upon whether the tax is upon real property, personal property, tangible or intangible property, inheritance, or income. In addition to these many ways of determining jurisdiction, a new difficulty arises in that the determination of these various ways is itself clouded by ambiguity and confusion due to conflicting purposes. Jurisdiction for purposes of multiple taxation will vary as we apply different principles of limitation upon the power of different states to tax the same individual because of the need to reconcile the conflicting interests of the states and the individual taxed.[26]

The problematic character of the meaning of an event, and the dependence of the answer upon notions of what is desirable, is illustrated outside of law as well as in law.

[26] See Union Refrigerator Transit Co. v. Kentucky, 199 U.S. 194 (1905); Johnson Oil Refining Co. v. Oklahoma, 290 U.S. 158 (1933); Farmers Loan and Trust Co. v. Minnesota, 280 U.S. 204 (1930); Blackstone v. Miller, 188 U.S. 189 (1930); Baldwin v. Missouri, 281 U.S. 586 (1930); First National Bank v. Maine, 284 U.S. 312 (1932); Lawrence v. State Tax Commission, 286 U.S. 276 (1932).

In law, however, it exists to such an extent that it virtually constitutes the essence of the "artificial reason" of the law. Such questions as who (or what) is a person, what is property, what constitutes negligence, when is an offer an offer "within the meaning of the law," and their devised answers are the stock in trade of the lawyer. The lawyer best able to answer rightly these questions persuasively in hard cases is said to be the most capable.[27]

The assumption that events bespeak their character by merely happening has made for many strange reasonings in the history of jurisprudence. Events have meaning, it is true, but the meaning is always potential, or rather there are many meanings relative to many purposes. A situation is potentially meaningful in many directions, and which meaning is relevant is in part dependent upon a human judgment.[28] A window may be an instrument for letting in light, an object to throw at, or something to make a profit on. These meanings are not autonomous and unrelated, and, moreover, they all depend upon events independent of the window.[29] Yet once we posit the "essence" of the window we are already well along on our problem of how to treat it. What we do about events will inevitably depend upon the meaning we give to them. It is not asserted that meanings and values are personal or arbitrary for any given situation. The common assumption of all writers who agree in substance with this position is that events for any one individual

[27] See Cook, *Facts and the Statement of Facts* (1937) 4 UNIVERSITY OF CHICAGO LAW REVIEW 233.

[28] Evidence of this is to be seen in the fact that considerable emphasis must be placed by anyone critically analyzing a case upon the manner in which the facts are stated. It is further suggested by the distinction between material and immaterial facts and the use made of this distinction by the courts, as well as by the distinction between law and fact. See Isaacs, *The Law and the Facts* (1922) 22 COLUMBIA LAW REVIEW 1.

[29] See WILLIAM JAMES, PSYCHOLOGY (1890) II, 332–40, on reasoning of which this is the particular legal application.

are for the most part given; they are socially defined not only as to possibilities of meaning but also as to the eminent character of some one meaning.

Similarly, for any particular judge on any particular occasion, conflicts which get into court are as such defined. To say that society gives us our categories and meanings, just as it may dictate our ends as well as our instruments, is, however, to say only that it offers the usual and habitual. But custom and tradition are precisely what are most frequently in need of critical judgment, as the traditional institution of judges testifies. The interdependence of ends, means, and meaning usually implies that the criticism, rejection, and alteration of accepted categories and meanings occur as a consequence of changes in the values involved.[30] In a sense, it is just this awareness of the need for such criticism which locates one fundamental emphasis of contemporary realistic jurisprudence.[31] There is certainly nothing unalterable about the meanings or values of situations as society gives them to the participating individual, and the point where criticism ought to be most in evidence is precisely in the activity of professional judges, whose business it is to settle "conflicts which do not otherwise get settled"[32] and whose aim it is to settle by reference to a general norm.

[30] A striking example of this in political philosophy is to be found in John Dewey's reinterpretations of freedom. See his FREEDOM AND CULTURE (1939).

[31] This is recognized by the insistence that judges frankly face the problem of evaluation in particular judgments. This is not to make every legal question wholly a question of "public policy," but it is to urge that where the questions of direct evaluation are involved they are to that extent to be directly faced. See Cohen, *Transcendental Nonsense and the Functional Approach* (1935) 35 COLUMBIA LAW REVIEW 809. Holmes anticipated this phase of contemporary legal realism in *The Path of the Law* in COLLECTED LEGAL PAPERS (1921) 186, 195.

[32] Llewellyn's conception of law and the legal process as essentially the pathological department of society puts neatly the emphasis needed to make judgment critical of what has been taken for granted. See his BRAMBLE BUSH (1930) 109 ff.

Not a little of contemporary criticism directed against traditional conceptions in the law is in essence a criticism of concepts that not only make for decisions in terms of values irrelevant to contemporary action but for further problems by virtue of the fact that resident in these concepts are many incompatible values.[33] To use ideas and perspectives so that they remain in truth more nearly what they are meant to be requires an ever-watchful eye and constant criticism.

THE PROBLEM OF UNITY

The fact that the use of precedent is itself based on precedent or tradition may indicate a continuity and unity which are more than merely historical or it may indicate merely the inertia of stimulus and response. Nothing that has been said is intended to be a denial of historical continuity. There is, indeed, a unity in precedent, but in practice it becomes evident that in many cases the unity is so difficult to "construct" that it seems to be wholly manufactured.[34] The evidence for unity other than a formal unity in many situations is nowhere nearly so great as for plurality, individuality, levels, or multiplicity of contexts, values, principles, standards, ends, and rights. Especially, situations calling for judgments are apt to be precisely those most conspicuous for competing and relatively unprecedented values.[35] The

[33] The attempt to reformulate some important categories in contract law on the basis of studies already made and on the basis of making the legal categories fit more clearly the value interests at stake is the task Llewellyn has undertaken. See *The Rule of Law in Our Case Law of Contracts* (1938) 47 YALE LAW JOURNAL 1243; *Our Case Law of Contract: Offer and Acceptance* (1938) 48 YALE LAW JOURNAL 1. The subject matter of this chapter is admirably covered in these articles, including the subjects of "conflict," "indeterminancy," "plurality," and the essential problematic character of judgment.

[34] Arnold, in his *Apologia for Jurisprudence* (1935) 44 YALE LAW JOURNAL 729, satirizes well this supposition of the unity of law and the effort to construct it.

[35] See Oliphant and Hewitt's Introduction to RUEFF, FROM THE PHYSICAL TO THE SOCIAL SCIENCES (1929) xvi.

synthetic unity when imposed by the judge may be said to be unreal; to be a genuine unity it must emerge in the particular conflict and not merely be applied to it. Law approached from this perspective makes necessary a situational analysis. Here "situation" is understood not as a defined datum but as a name for the problematic context or the copresence of distinguishable contexts, ranges of universality and meaning, and types of values potentially at issue.

The theory of justice and of legal evaluation surely includes a concern for this ultimate unity considered from the point of view of the search for a general end or standard, but it is not required as a basic postulate for procedure. The problems of justice, being problems of judgment, are clearly centered around specific conflicts and values; criteria applied to these specific situations in order to define their proper context are the most problematic factors. The unity of justice, no matter how firmly it may be believed or however well expressed by catchall contexts of rights, is of little help in the quest for the just solution to a particular problem. Given such a unity it is of small help in the consideration of what delay ought to be permitted in the shipping of cantaloupe from Colorado to New York. In some situations it may be very important, but the mere fact that dialectically we may raise the general problem of justice in any situation does not thereby render it the important context. Because *the* end of the law by definition subsumes all other ends of the law, one may not wisely decide situations by reference to a too inclusive context or value, when such a reference distorts the relative value of the lesser contexts. "The famous three principles of Ulpian, 'live honourably,' 'injure no one,' 'give each man his due,' are succinct enough in all conscience, but that they will guide us in the simplest of litigated causes is hard to believe."[36] Every appeal to an ultimate must be justified realistically in other than ultimate terms. The instrumental value of a *ratio decidendi* that is merely an ultimate principle has rarely been high. What value it has is as a symbol, and when used as an instrument it becomes a mere device.

INSTRUMENTS AND DEVICES

The distinction between an "instrument" and a "device" needs clarification since ordinarily we do not make any important distinction between the two terms. It resembles the distinction between a rationale and a rationalization, between a scientific statement and a myth, between analysis and rhetoric. If a technical rule of procedure is applied to a problem of procedure, it functions as an instrument for that situation, but if the same technical rule of procedure is used to decide a problem not essentially procedural in significance, though involving the point of procedure to which the rule is indeed applicable, that rule is used as a device.[37] Rules properly to be used within their intended context are often smuggled in to decide larger issues implying other contexts and when so used are termed devices or fictions. The use of the term fiction indicates usually a flagrant use of devices. Neither the term fiction[38] nor the term device is meant of itself to carry a moral connotation. A device receives its moral character in the particular situation in which it is used, for good or evil as the case may be. But

[36] Radin, *The Education of a Lawyer* (1937) 25 CALIFORNIA LAW REVIEW 687–88.

[37] See Lorenzen, Phelps, and Heilman, *The Restatement of the Conflict of Laws* (1935) 83 UNIVERSITY OF PENNSYLVANIA LAW REVIEW 555, 564, for a criticism of the restatement on the ground that it fails to give recognition to the important use of conflict of law doctrine to decide substantive matters and assumes that it is only a procedural matter of defining which law is applicable.

[38] For an excellent treatment of legal fictions, see Fuller, *Legal Fictions* (1930) 25 ILLINOIS LAW REVIEW 363, 513, 877.

like the term fiction, it tends to designate an intellectual evasion. Thus Corwin, discussing the Schechter case[39] and the distinction drawn by the opinion between "direct and indirect" effects of intrastate activity on the movement of interstate commerce, calls that distinction a "verbal device" with an evident tone of moral censure.[40] Similarly, Jeremy Bentham's excoriations against the use of abstractions and "fictions" have a decidedly adverse evaluation implied in the use of the term. Those who think of the categories of crime simply as categories into which acts of violence fit are not likely to approve the use of these categories as bargaining points between the prosecutor and the criminal or as formulae apportioning possible punishment as the needs of the criminal vary;[41] in either case it is true they are using instruments as devices, whether in a morally reprehensible way or merely as intellectual short cuts. The use of devices cannot be condemned a priori, because as a general technique it has been not only indispensable but inevitable, given the legal and social situation. The contemporary recognition of the impossibility of a judge merely applying rules, of being merely a "mouthpiece" of the law, is in part a recognition of the special techniques available to the court, of which the use of precedent as a device is not the least important.

This use of precedent as a device has significance for the discussion of precedent as an illustration of the categorical character of the problematic and indeterminate nature of contexts and of their radical plurality. For what makes us conscious of the fact that the unity of justice is more nominal than real is the frequent manipulation of

[39] Schechter Poultry Corp. v. United States, 257 U.S. 342 (1935).

[40] *The Schechter Case* in LAW, A CENTURY OF PROGRESS (1937) II, 32–37.

[41] See MOLEY, POLITICS AND CRIMINAL PROSECUTION (1929). See also Tulin, *The Role of Penalties in Criminal Law* (1928) 37 YALE LAW JOURNAL 1048.

devices in a plurality of contexts. Verbally, judges have discovered unity of doctrine and principle; actually, this "discovery" is the result of clever manipulation to avoid recognition of a more obvious plurality or even conflict. The consciousness of the role of precedents as "pegs to hang one's case on" is only another way of recognizing the essential multiplicity of context and the problematic character of reference to precedents as a body of possibilities and suggestions. Principles in precedent, like trees, have small beginnings, and the growth of a single precedent to a basic principle is a growth from a fruitful instrument to what may also be used as a fruitful symbolic device. That it is palpably used as a device and not only as a genuine instrument throws light on the character of unity in law considered either as to end or as to criterion.

CONFLICT

The correlative principle of plurality and multiplicity of contexts in the interpretation and analysis of conflicts is the relative indeterminateness of the conflict. The correlative to both is the principle of conflict among contexts. Planes of reference have meaning and use to the extent that they enlighten deliberation, to the extent that they aid in directing mediation, adjustment, and decision. Such is their genesis, and such is their function. If all contexts led in one direction indiscriminately, their contextual reference would be futile. They do not precisely because the context is always a value context, and different contexts, to be different, must throw emphasis upon different value considerations. In such situations, conflict and competition are as basic between contexts as they are within contexts and as ineradicable as plurality. The jockeying for position by advocates in stating the facts of the conflict to be judged is a preliminary skirmish of utmost importance in the effort to persuade the judge to see the facts legally, that is, in terms of particular legal contexts, so chosen that the "proper" values—those favorable to the particular advocate—will dominate judgment.[42] "These are the facts; is it or is it not interstate commerce? Is it or is it not an affair of states rights? Is it property, or is it contract?" The man offered, but is there an "offer"? These are the familiar questions in terms of which decisions are made. To formulate the "facts" in one way and not in the other is to get one kind of a decision and not another.[43]

The greater the distance between the fact and the "legal fact," the more clearly is the legal fact seen to be the valuation of the fact. To imprint the context "contract" upon an agreement is to set off a chain of consequences which ends in a judgment. Andrews, in his dissenting opinion in the Palsgraf Case,[44] rests his argument on a frank recognition that a "proximate cause" in law is an evaluation in terms of public policy of the extent to which an individual, in strict fact a partial cause of an injury, is to be held liable. Every context of interpretation, whether legal or social, is more or less a value context,[45] and the legal context, which is merely a name of an evaluation, differs only in degree of explicitness from a formal nonevaluative context. The problem of identifying contexts becomes one of "constructing" contexts or choosing values and marking the evaluation.

[42] In this connection, consider the distinction between material and immaterial facts and also the many rules governing the admission of evidence. See Arnold, *The Role of Substantive Law and Procedure in the Legal Process* (1932) 45 HARVARD LAW REVIEW 617.

[43] See Cook, *"Facts" and the "Statement of Facts"* (1937) 4 UNIVERSITY OF CHICAGO LAW REVIEW 233.

[44] Palsgraf v. Long Island R. Co., 248 N. Y. 339 (1928).

[45] CARDOZO, THE PARADOXES OF LEGAL SCIENCE (1928) 75: "Back of the answers [to what the law is] is a measurement of interests, a balancing of values, an appeal to the experience and sentiments and moral and economic judgments of the community, the group, the trade."

We may summarize the discussion to this point. The extent to which law is uncertain; issues relatively indeterminate; possible issues and rules applicable to those issues in conflict or confused; particular judgments semi-autonomous, situationally localized, plural, and particular have been given less attention in our consideration of both law and justice than these matters deserve. Instead of accepting these features as accidental or irrelevant, they need emphasis as essential traits of the legal process, as evident and as important as those traits which philosophies of law have usually emphasized. The process of legal judgment, as it is empirically observed, involves the use of rules and principles for a clarification of what the law is and what the issue presented for judgment may be treated as. This involves, in greater or less degree, a consideration of possible rules applicable to the case, of the conclusions of the case which would eventuate, and of the merits both of rules applicable and of their net effect on the particular case. The attempt to determine what the law is involves a simultaneous attempt to determine what is desirable. We turn then to values and valuations as they operate in the actual process of legal judgment.

VALUES AND RIGHTS

Law is an instrument for the public adjustment of private disputes; this adjustment is known as adjudication. It works in two directions: in the interest of the particular disputants and in the interest of some larger group or groups.[46] Individuals resort to courts for the settlement of grievances after other means have failed in

[46] BENTLEY, THE PROCESS OF GOVERNMENT (1908), is convinced that the former is reducible in every instance to the latter. See also DEWEY, THE PUBLIC AND ITS PROBLEMS (1927). CARDOZO, THE JURISDICTION OF THE COURT OF APPEALS (1903) 11, is suggestive here: "The court exists . . . for the indefinite body of litigants whose causes are potentially involved in the specific cause at issue."

the same way that they take advantage of hospital facilities provided by health insurance after exhausting the home medicine cabinet for cures. The second general interest is the interest of groups in the particular conflict, an interest generated by the effect disputes have upon the welfare of those indirectly concerned. This public interest, though frequently identified with criminal law, is equally associated with civil law. Law always reflects a public interest in particular grievances, because if conflict is overt, though it involves only two individuals or groups, it constitutes potential danger to the community. Beyond this, particular grievances have always been indicia of conditions that make for more grievances, and, if only in the interest of self-preservation, such conditions cannot wisely be ignored. Thus, justice as a collective term for adjustment is both private and public.

Law does not achieve a permanent order, and inevitably it is concerned with what Llewellyn aptly calls "eternal problems." It is because we eternally have problems that we require professional adjusters. The major focus of the most vital problems in legal judgment is the presence of conflicts which are conflicts of ways, each of which is right to one party but offends the other.[47] In such situations, adjudication between groups, each representing norms which are guides in action, can at best be adjustment by compromise. Where each follows his own ways as right, and where the purposes and ways of each conflict, the situation can be dealt with only by getting the parties "to pull in their horns" in order to make way for one another. This is never wholly an affair of sanction by force, for effective adjustment is essentially noncoercible. The sanction, as Thomas Aquinas among others long ago urged, is primarily and basically an affair of right-

[47] Cohen, *The Problems of Functional Jurisprudence* (1937) 1 MODERN LAW REVIEW 15, 21; HALL, THEFT, LAW AND SOCIETY (1935) Chapter VI.

ness.[48] And so arises the problem of reworking and re-adapting mutually conflicting patterns. This is a process that is neither wholly confined to law nor yet to social actions explicitly outside of law. It is a process that occurs in both. Old antagonistic rights are constantly integrated in new intergroup relations, just as new classes of independently developing rights and systems of rights are constantly emerging. Always and ever this problem of adjustment faces law. Indeed, the basic effort of law—in short, justice—may be said to be this effort to adjust concrete interests.

This basic fact is only emphasized when laws and their purposes are looked at in terms of relatively formal and formulated rights and duties, instead of in simple terms of precedent or in terms of the social process. The approach to law through the conception of rights and duties is a limited approach because it fails as such to give recognition to the problem of the genesis of rights; it places that character of social operation in the past tense. Nevertheless, it has value not only in that rights and duties are indeed in the language of the law but, for our purposes, because it indicates just as well the ingrained plural and problematic character of law and justice with respect to values.

A nominalistic analysis might assert that a right could exist only after it is enforced and no rights could be said to exist prior to this enforcement. As such, each right must perforce be individual and unique. As an assertion simply about what is, a right would be a recognition of the tautology that what has been has been. It is, however, another matter to recognize with the realist that while rights are claims that have been protected or enforced by events, or for which the courts have provided a remedy, such rights when stated categorically are under-

[48] SABINE, A HISTORY OF POLITICAL THEORY (1937) 248 ff.

standable as shorthand expressions, as clues to predictions, of what courts are likely to do in the future.[49] Rights as assertions of what courts have done become predictions of what they will do under similar circumstances. Rights are neither wholly future nor wholly past nor both together; they are present aids for the guidance of future action.[50] Fruitful thought about rights begins when the right is oriented with respect to future action. "A right is as big, precisely, as what the courts will do."[51] A right is an affair of the future, and for the individual who claims the right it is an affair of probability.

Rights as predictions can never be certain; they approach such certainty as an asymptote the more they are framed in concrete and limited terms.[52] Given a merely verbal unification, the possibility of accurate prediction is to that extent lessened. When the particular matter is subsumed under a completely unified conception, the predictions made thereon are of small value.[53] In short, no lawyer worthy of a fee bases a prediction on a principle alone. Rights, conceived as predictions of remedial action by the legal mechanism on behalf of a claimant, to be effective must be plurally conceived, though not so singularly as to be absolutely particular. This implies two things equally. On the one hand, rights are not merely particular—which would mean each right being only the

[49] Cook, *Scientific Method and Law* (1927) 13 AMERICAN BAR ASSOC. JOURNAL 303.

[50] We are excluding at present an idealistic conception of rights.

[51] LLEWELLYN, THE BRAMBLE BUSH (1930) 82.

[52] Yet even so specified for the individual case a particular space-time locus creates a situation wherein chance factors operate. The particular court, judge, lawyer, party, occasion, and the like are canceled out in statistical thinking about the matter of rights but can not wisely be forgotten by the individual who seeks to establish this right practically. See, for example, Hutcheson, *Lawyers, Law and the Little Small Dice* (1932) 7 TULANE LAW REVIEW 1; ULMAN, A JUDGE TAKES THE STAND (1933).

[53] Oliphant, *The Return to Stare Decisis* (1928) 14 AMERICAN BAR ASSOC. JOURNAL 71, 72.

right it is and nothing more—on the other hand, this construction of rights in terms of probability emphasizes the fact that the unity and integration of rights does not go so far as to constitute a universal and certain system of rights culminating in the universal right or standard of right which subsumes all the others and from which the others may be deduced.

To orient discussion solely in terms of prediction is to take the counselor's position and not the judge's. Prediction as such is correct or incorrect, and the future does or does not verify the prediction. But even from the point of view of prediction, the question of what is held as right by the legal personnel, where right is taken however ambiguously as a proper claim, is an important factor in any analysis. A counselor's or an advocate's analysis cannot ignore the claims of rightness and decency that will be brought to bear upon a possibly disputed case.[54] How a judge will react to the merits needs measurement. A rule or principle that presents some probability of appealing to the court as in accordance with needs of the situation is to that extent more dependable than if it lacks such appeal. Yet fruitful analysis of values, which within the situation are likely to impress the judge as desirable, must be sufficiently concrete to make a difference. The more general the value, the less discriminating force will it have in illuminating possible courses of action.[55] Almost any concrete legal situation is an illustration of this. Rights, perceived by lawyers as instruments of prediction, indicate their relative multiplicity and problematic character. Rights, conceived by judges and legislators as pres-

[54] See Cohen, *The Problems of Functional Jurisprudence* (1937) 1 MODERN LAW REVIEW 5, 13: "There is need even in these narrow questions for social vision."

[55] Oliphant, *The Return to Stare Decisis* (1928) 14 AMERICAN BAR ASSOC. JOURNAL 181: "Generalization is necessary but over generalization is useless and vicious."

ent realities and norms, indicate no less indeterminateness, complexity, and multiple contexts.

It is possible to distinguish at least three aspects in the idea of a legal right: the claim urged, the known or projected consequences which are held to validate the claim, and, assuming a validated claim, the remedy available.[56] The remedial right is the practical instrument of protection and of enforcement, without which law would be exhortation and a right an academic matter. "Absence of remedy is absence of right." A substantive right, or the claim itself, is, when properly presented to the court, a stimulus inducing action by the court, and that action is by means of, and in terms of, the remedial right. The validation of the claim in terms of foreseen consequences and approved ends and standards transforms the claim into a legal right and creates the need for the creation of the remedial right. To consider law as a system of rights and duties and justice as the protection of rights and the enforcement of duties is to assume the presence of all three parts.

But considering law in these terms and approaching it empirically, one finds both integrated systems of rights and duties as well as conflicts between and within systems. The conflict, for example, between justice as a matter of inexorable retribution and as in essence an affair of an approximately equitable result is, it would seem, "eternal." Both apparently have been in the history of thought, regarded as essential to a completely adequate law, yet neither permits the full extension of the other. The question may be raised as to whether this conflict

[56] A full analysis would, of course, be much more involved than this and would not involve such ambiguity in the use of the term "right." For one realist's interest in adequate analysis, see Radin, *A Restatement of Hohfeld* (1938) 51 HARVARD LAW REVIEW 1141. See also Goble, *A Redefinition of Basic Legal Terms* (1935) 35 COLUMBIA LAW REVIEW 535. Goble treats the progressive parts as phases of the basic idea, power-liability.

and others of a similar nature are not after all verbal. It may well be that this conflict is the result of attempting to use intellectual tools of insufficient discriminating force. Yet the almost necessary use of concepts such as "adjustment" and "balancing" in describing efforts to realize justice gives evidence of the fact that somewhere along the line actual conflicts are present in aims or in procedures. These general conflicts may not be vital issues in conflict, but there is at least the possibility that they reflect an ongoing process wherein the expansion of some interests are at the expense of restricting others with consequent strife and uncertainty. An illustration of the coexistence of interests is to be found in the assumptions made regarding crime. The interest in dealing effectively with a criminal is primarily a matter of efficiency. Yet the most efficient methods are limited in their application because they are in conflict with the interest in "human rights." The use of torture as a method of obtaining confessions works, particularly when the statements elicited are accompanied by verification. By rejecting such methods, we cripple effective procedures in criminal law and believe such rejection to be well worth the sacrifice.[57] Apparent conflict is by no means confined to such general issues. The opposition of methods of action applicable to the same situation may be illustrated throughout the law.

> Legal principles have a habit of running in pairs, a plaintiff principle and a defendant principle . . . in law one generally has a choice between opposite "principles." Writers of legal treatises have no compunction about setting two principles side by side with only a "but" or "however" between them for the sake of decency.[58]

[57] See Arnold's stimulating presentation of the contradictions of the ideal of law enforcement, *Law Enforcement—an Attempt at Social Dissection* (1932) 42 YALE LAW JOURNAL 1, 8 ff.

[58] Cohen, *The Problems of Functional Jurisprudence* (1937) 1 MODERN LAW REVIEW 10–11. See also Yntema, *The Hornbook Method and the*

The law permits the government to refuse the use of the mails; the law also permits the publishing of lottery tickets. The exercise of the one is used, in effect, to deprive the other of its effectiveness, and we have the lottery cases.[59] The law permits workers to organize, and the law permits employers to dismiss; we have our famous labor cases of recent years.[60] The law permits the government to let its contracts mostly on its own conditions, and industries maintain they have the right to employ men at whatever wages they can get them to work for; the enforcement of one of the opposing rights limits the other.[61] Litigations in court are preëminently affairs of defense and attack in terms of different systems of legally formulated interests. The rights need not logically contradict one another, but the choice of one pattern does, in fact, result in the repudiation of the other for the case in hand.[62]

PERMANENCE AND CHANGE

The inertia and permanence which characterize present rights are partially functions of the strength of the vested interests involved. Even though the mobility in property law has increased in recent years, the rights of real property remain relatively unchanged and the statutes of

---

Conflict of Laws (1928) 37 YALE LAW JOURNAL 468; Llewellyn, *The Rule of Law in Our Case Law of Contract* (1938) 47 YALE LAW JOURNAL 1243, 1249 ff., especially 1253; Eno, *Price Movements and Unstated Objections to the Defective Performance of Sales Contracts* (1935) 44 YALE LAW JOURNAL 782.

[59] See, for example, *ex parte* Jackson, 96 U.S. 727 (1878).

[60] See, for example, Coppage v. Kansas, 236 U.S. 1 (1915); Adair v. United States, 208 U.S. 161 (1908); Texas and New Orleans R. Co. v. Brotherhood of Ry. and S.S. Clerks, 281 U.S. 548 (1930).

[61] HALE, *On Conditional Withholding of Privileges*, LEGAL FACTORS IN ECONOMIC SOCIETY (1937) 79 ff.

[62] The layman is less aware of this than the lawyer because of the techniques available for whittling away at established rules for decision. Cf. the use of these techniques in Knight and Dosnick v. Moore, 203 Wis. 540 (1931), and cases cited by Llewellyn, *The Rule of Law in Our Case Law of Contract* (1938) 47 YALE LAW JOURNAL 1249.

Clarendon, of Elizabeth, and of Henry VIII offer some of the most vital definitions of a right of property today. The permanence and harmony of existing property rights are functions, to a considerable extent, of their very plurality and specificity. In no field are the procedures, rights, and standards so clear-cut and concrete as in this field. Knowledge of the laws of property is more technical than knowledge in other fields of law. Counseling is here a much more certain enterprise. If proof were needed for the assertion that effectiveness both of prediction and evaluation is to a great extent a function of the clearness and distinctness of the instruments of prediction and the subject matter of evaluation, it would be found here. In property law, kinds and classes and distinctions are given for almost every conceivable transaction.

What is true in property law is also true, but to a lesser extent, in other fields. The rights in law are there. The pressure upon the laws of property by interests and claims not yet recognized must be so much greater than in other phases of law that except interstitially property laws remain unchanged and judgments about property are primarily administrative. The nature of the interests at stake in property law has made for greater explicitness and a more concrete body of rights than one finds in the other categories. Legal rights in real property are internally, at least, our most consistent body of rights. The extent to which there exists a conflict between established legal rights is much less in evidence here than in the other fields of interest in the law. Yet even here the effect of sit-down strikes in raising the question as to what a property right is makes it apparent that pressures sufficiently strong do threaten to cut in upon the established system of property rights.

But the consistency in this field differs only in degree from the workable consistency in other fields. For while in the above paragraphs we have been reviewing essential conflicts between interests, engendered by change, multiple tendencies, and pressures, such a position by no means implies complete chaos. Consistency and harmony are as much in evidence as conflict and antagonism. It is because the body of law has the harmony and integration it has that it creates or makes more acute the problem of moving with the needs and new directions of society, thus creating perpetual problems of justice. Rights pregnantly illustrate the fact that ideas whose origin is in utility take their place with established rights and are integrated into a system. The layman's difficulty and displeasure with the law come from the fact that he frequently does not appreciate the inertia that resides in a coördinated system of rights. The entrance of any new claim into the family of existing rights or the destruction of an existing harmful right must overcome the inertia given to an established right by the fact that being established it is more or less integrated into the total body. The recognition of a new right or new direction affects not only some rights that must give way; it affects, either by implication or directly, the whole pattern. Here, too, the impact of sit-down strikes upon the rights of property was not on a few property rights only; the present controversy may well affect the whole pattern of property rights. The question it raises, for example, of the extent to which private property involves pertinent and real public responsibility touches every property right now in force. The impact is resisted, therefore, by the whole pattern to the extent that the integration exists. This is one of the important reasons why an integrated body of rights like that of real property is so effective, so permanent, and, therefore, so dangerous. But even in property law, direction is evident.[63] For law is not only a process; it is in

[63] See, for example, Niles, *The Law of Estates since Butler and Kent* in LAW, A CENTURY OF PROGRESS, 1835–1935 (1937) III, 199.

process as well. One need only inspect the history of the living American Constitution to see the significance of movement as a categorical characteristic of law and justice.[64] Justice is included in law as its "jural end" and is an affair of expansion and contraction, of growth and decay, of construction and reconstruction.[65] Rights and duties and standards and values form the elements that change. Seen in terms of movement, justice represents tendencies which are practically embodied in part in terms of pressures. These pressures are not all of a kind and they not only diverge but compete as well. Law in responding to felt needs meets with contrary or disparate established rights and pressures, and it is the effective adjustment of each to each with a minimum of friction that makes good judgment difficult but fortunately not too rare.

Change in law and in justice is only emphasized by the fact that rules of law and norms of decision continue to have a technical authoritative and frequently influential status even after actual decisions have expanded contrary rules and rights into *de facto* established positions. In law

> the stream determines its own banks; the rules are merely [in the first instance] a statement of the uniformity of the stream [of actual decision], and they are continually undermined and reëstablished elsewhere as the tide of decision ebbs and flows with the needs, feelings, and desires of mankind.[66]

That a chose in action—that is, a creditor's right against his debtor—could not be assigned was the spoken law and in certain procedures the norm enforced for almost

[64] See Llewellyn, *The Constitution as an Institution* (1934) 34 COLUMBIA LAW REVIEW 1, for an excellent discussion of the "living constitution."

[65] CARDOZO, THE PARADOXES OF LEGAL SCIENCE (1928) 41: "There must be flexibility for a formula that will hold within its walls this thing of changing content. Justice as a jural norm is not a fixed or determinate phase of the totality of moral conduct within a given situation."

[66] Corbin, *Contracts for the Benefit of Third Persons* (1931) 46 LAW QUARTERLY REVIEW 12.

a hundred years or more after its contrary—that such rights could be assigned—had been recognized in other modes of procedure. The same was essentially true in recent years of the right of a third party beneficiary to sue on the contract. Altered situations in fact pressed upon stable ways of treating this triangular situation to effect an almost complete reversal of decision, of norm, and, consequently, of rights.

The substance of justice, namely, the judgments made upon law and by law, has a history. The movement which occurs among these purposes and needs is frequently obscured by the very stability of the language which embodies them and the techniques we have for obscuring that change. Within the system of law, the clue to change is given by language in the form of "implementation" and similar devices. The treatment given the formula "let the buyer beware" (*caveat emptor*) is an eminent illustration of this. An apparent uniformity in the application of this formula is discoverable in the cases. Yet law is always finding "unique" situations where justice is not obtainable by the strict use of the formula and either explicitly or by means of various techniques —for example, the doctrine of implied warranty—distinctions are drawn separating out this kind of case from other cases. When the law recognizes that the multiplications of exceptions have in effect qualified the principle out of existence, a new principle is formulated which makes of all the exceptions a new uniformity.

This whole process is obscured by the language used.[67] For qualifications of rules represent a successful competition of one claim, procedure, or standard as against another. The qualifications come after the general end or

[67] CARDOZO, THE PARADOXES OF LEGAL SCIENCE (1928) 10: "We may think the law is the same if we refuse to change the formulae. The identity is verbal only."

rule is established, yet they are often described as qualifications which have existed since the inception of the rule. In analogous fashion there is the constant subsumption of novel cases under existing formulae while refusing to recognize that the formulae themselves are changed by virtue of their new content. The whole language of "qualification," of "implementation," and of "interpretation" is in essence a manner of pointing out the acceptance of different standards and a refusal clearly to recognize it. This is not a "penalty" but a "tax." The "liberty" protected by the Constitution is not "license." Similar statements have been the language in which powers previously exercised and rights protected, in short, elements of justice, were quietly put to death. The "cutting in" on existing rules heralds the presence of new standards for these concrete occasions.

The presence of new aims and new standards means the emergence of claims heretofore unrecognized and the presence of pressures which have gathered strength. The "moral norm" has been transferred into a "jural norm." As what ought to be, justice is an interest in these claims which press for recognition. It thus has a temporal dimension which expresses itself in multiple tendencies and directions; it has, therefore, nonlegal or only potentially legal content as well. This content is essentially characterized by movement and change as well as by permanence and structure. The values by which we judge particular incidents and disputes are from the first multiple and constantly in process. Although that which puts order in the changing, and gives those changes a direction, is not for that reason in change itself, the values by which we guide action do themselves have a direction, a growth, and an essentially transitional character. The contents of justice have life careers which are more than a sequence of unrelated parts. Justice is a matter both of structures and of processes. Viewed only as an abstract structure, justice is distorted; it is equally distorted when seen not in process but simply in flux. Though justice ideally may be one, yet, as empirically known, it is at best a collective unity, composed of rights, interests, claims, pressures, and values which are both integrated, independent, and, even in some cases, in competition. To say that justice has a temporal character means just this impact of value upon value, of growth here at the expense of decay somewhere else. Its total substantive unity, if it has such, is not known, and what is known renders doubtful even its possibility. As unknown, it is irrelevant for practical judgment. Empirical judgment operates with the "probably satisfactory" and not with eternal verities. "We need not ask ourselves whether justice is eternal or unchanging. Eternity is a long word and lawyers have long ago supplied themselves with temporal notions that will serve as substitutes for eternity."[68]

"Is it possible," asks Cardozo, "that in rationalizing . . . we have been hampered by . . . [an] illusion? We have sought for a formula consistent with a steady advance through a continuum. The continuum does not exist."[69] Cardozo is asserting that every new case is always more or less a shot in the dark and a matter of adjustment; there are no ultimate principles from which can be derived other principles which in turn measure justice and injustice in particular situations. Decisions reflect the pull of many values and standards and a decision comes to rest usually between two poles. "Centers of energy exist, of attraction and repulsion. A landing place is found between them. We make these landing places for ourselves through the methods of the judicial process."[70]

[68] Radin, *The Education of a Lawyer* (1937) 25 CALIFORNIA LAW REVIEW 676, 688.

[69] THE PARADOXES OF LEGAL SCIENCE (1928) 4.

[70] *Ibid.*

Justice, empirically viewed, assumes the appearance of a collective concept open at both ends with a membership list of rights and pressures that is constantly changing.[71] Law is not, nor ought it to be, ever completely sure of the character of any one member. Membership therein is always on good behavior. Old members sometimes stay long after they have served their usefulness and the grounds which made them members have long departed. New members fail of admittance frequently because of cliques of old members who oppose them. But membership is never absolute, neither in time nor in authority. No member is a member except in the perspective and context which made it a member. This is the character of justice in its empirical content as we meet it in the courts.

[71] See Harper, *Some Implications of Juristic Pragmatism* (1929) 39 INTERNATIONAL JOURNAL OF ETHICS 269, 281.

CHAPTER III

THE INDETERMINATE IN JUSTICE

UNTIL NOW we have been concerned with the results of a realistic analysis of the judicial processes as they affect the more concrete aspects of justice. Viewed in terms of cases, precedents, rules, and particular decisions, justice, adjectivally rather than substantivally conceived, is attached to innumerable activities which together make up the body of functioning law. We have attempted to make explicit the characteristics of justice in this context. The clue to these characteristics lies in the recognition that while the attribute "just" qualifies a decision, rule, or result, it does not make them any more or less decisions, rules, and concrete results. The essential qualities and characteristics which attach to any decision attach with equal force to just decisions. The attribution of the quality of being just to a decision denotes an evaluation of a decision, but it also, and for our purpose more importantly, clarifies the concrete characteristics of justice.

Justice has, however, other facets, namely, its connections with general principles, standards, ends, and ideals which are usually considered primary in assays of justice. The following chapters will be concerned with some of the existing formulations of the principles and standards of justice. Our interest is not in the further formulation of new ideals and standards but in the clarification of the nature and operation of the principles and standards that are current.

Judges find need for general formulae which direct attention to the larger issues or more fundamental themes than the immediate problems at hand. The formulae in American law that have come to play this role both together and alone are such phrases as police power, public policy, reasonableness, equal protection, and due process. It is in the use of these formulae in decisions that one would naturally expect to demonstrate the reality or the force of justice as a determinate ideal or standard possessing that clarity, precision, and generality required to make a difference on its own account in decisions by courts; here, if anywhere, one might expect a formula of justice to show its worth as a guide to decisions. That these formulae do not function as thus indicated but, on the contrary, illustrate an almost amorphous elasticity is easily demonstrated by even a limited survey of their use.

THE APPEAL TO REASON

The conception of the reasonable has long been a major instrument for enlarging the context of reference in American law. Its power to widen the horizon of deliberation is attested to by its many appearances in both private and public law as the receptacle and instrument of "fundamental rights."[1] Though not a textual stipulation of the United States Constitution, the reasonable constitutes the vital principle in considerations of due process of law, equal protection, police power,[2] and, in general, all the important phrases and doctrines which determine the validity of legislative and administrative acts.[3] It has special applications in such matters as rea-

[1] See Reeder, *Constitutional and Extra-Constitutional Restraints* (1913) 61 UNIVERSITY OF PENNSYLVANIA LAW REVIEW 441, 452 ff.

[2] HAINES, THE REVIVAL OF NATURAL LAW CONCEPTS (1930) Chapter VII.

[3] Reeder, *Is Unreasonable Legislation Unconstitutional?* (1914) 62 UNIVERSITY OF PENNSYLVANIA LAW REVIEW 191. See COMMONS, THE LEGAL FOUNDATIONS OF CAPITALISM (1924) Preface. The statement in the text is not essentially altered by the adoption in recent decisions of the Supreme

sonable action in restraint of trade, fair competition in business transactions, reasonable conduct in the law of negligence, reasonable return in public utility rates, reasonableness of taxes, and reasonableness in the exercise of eminent domain.[4] It is a commonplace that the contexts and applications of the standard of reasonableness are legion. Certainly any idea to which the conception of justice has been pertinent may be treated in terms of reason. Reasonableness is the legal counterpart to a philosophical conception of justice.

The appeal to reasonableness both in law and in jurisprudence is frequently in the context of an appeal from, and in opposition to, some existing state of affairs. For example, the appeal to reasonableness in the form it assumed in earlier times, namely, an appeal to some form of "the eternal principles of reason," was made in opposition to the claims of positive law or some feature of the existing law.[5] On the other hand, its exemplification in tort law and negligence cases as the appeal to the "reasonable man" and in popular speech the exhortation "be reasonable" mean in part, at least, an appeal to criteria that are not too ideal.[6] These phrases amount essentially to the demand that standards be relevant and an aid to practical or effective deliberation and judgment. At times,

---

Court of the United States of the "presumption of constitutionality," since this presumption is a presumption of reasonableness. See, for example, the opinion of the majority (Brandeis) in O'Gorman and Young v. Hartford Fire Ins. Co., 282 U.S. 251, 51 Sup. Ct. 130 (1931); Osborn v. Uzlin, 60 Sup. Ct. 758 (1940).

[4] For a brief review of the range of application of the concept in particular fields, see Harper, *Forms of Law and Moral Content* (1927) 22 ILLINOIS LAW REVIEW 259, 269 ff. See also the various RESTATEMENTS OF LAW, by the American Law Institute, for example, RESTATEMENT, CONTRACTS (1932) Sections 28, 32, 40 (offer expires "at the end of a reasonable time"). The range of application is almost unlimited.

[5] Dewey, *Nature and Reason in Law* (1914) 25 INTERNATIONAL JOURNAL OF ETHICS 25. See also his article in CREATIVE INTELLIGENCE (1917).

[6] See RESTATEMENT OF THE LAW OF TORTS (1934) Sections 289, 298, 299, 300, J. H. Bohlen, reporter, American Law Institute.

the reasonable is a device to effect an escape from a crystallized system of criteria or rules of analysis and of judgment which do not work justice. In other circumstances, the reasonable is neither an escape to ideals or principles nor from ideals and normative principles which render the achievement of justice precarious in the particular situation; rather, it functions so as to set an inquiry into contexts which are not so much legal as economic, political, and, in general, social contexts. It operates to instigate investigation into modes of action, the consequences of proposed judgments, and it permits survey both of the widest ideals and the most unique circumstances.

To testify to these functions of the reasonable in law is to point to the infinite elasticity of the conception and to its limitations as an operative factor in law in any other ways than those indicated. It is generally agreed that it is not a principle which may be said to determine either broad or specific issues. The following excerpt from a case involving the question of reasonable restraint of trade is significant:

> Reasonableness is not a concept of definite and unchanging content. Its meaning necessarily varies in the different fields of law, because it is used as a convenient summary of the dominant considerations which control in the application of legal doctrines. . . . We should hesitate to adopt a construction making the difference between legal and illegal conduct in the field of business relations depend upon so uncertain a test as whether prices are reasonable—a determination which can satisfactorily be made only after a complete survey of our economic organization and a choice between rival philosophies.[7]

Likewise, the commentators find "reasonableness" an indefinite guide:

[7] Stone in United States v. Trenton Potteries Co., 273 U.S. 392 (1927). See Brown, *Due Process of Law, Police Power and the Supreme Court* (1927) 40 HARVARD LAW REVIEW 943; Powell, *The Judiciality of Minimum Wage Legislation* (1924) 37 HARVARD LAW REVIEW 545.

It is submitted that up to the present time very little can be learned . . . from the decisions of the Supreme Court as to what in its judgment is reasonable and what is unreasonable. They neither give us a rule of law nor a definition.[8]

To look for a clear standard in any concept like reasonableness which has its application in such an elastic range of materials as the law presents is to find only many standards which are frequently in opposition. "There is certainly no principle of law to be found in this mass of contradictions."[9] Of all ideas that have successfully laid claim to represent most fully the nature of justice, the conception of reason is probably the most variable and relative. It is always a question of reasonableness under what circumstances and reasonableness to whom and for what.

Despite its relativity and its elasticity and despite the fact that taken as a single idea it comprises a multitude of irreconcilable attitudes, there is little question respecting its power and its relevance to law. Its power and its relevance are not, however, as a substantive standard. As a collective aggregate of notions, it contains many attitudes, valuable in their time and contexts and useful in their discriminating powers; as a category, it is one par excellence of approval after evaluation, which fact accounts for the presence in the collective conception of the reasonableness of many valuable and pertinent principles of law.[10] These principles are not, however, derived from it. Its use as a category of approval demands an explana-

[8] Willis, *Due Process of Law under the United States Constitution* (1926) 74 UNIVERSITY OF PENNSYLVANIA LAW REVIEW 331, 338; cited in HAINES, THE REVIVAL OF NATURAL LAW CONCEPTS (1930) 195.

[9] Barnett, *External Evidence of the Constitutionality of Statutes* (1924) 58 AMERICAN LAW REVIEW 88.

[10] See FREUND, STANDARDS OF AMERICAN LEGISLATION (1917) 5: "The criterion of reasonableness may be the only one available, but if so, it means that adequate scientific or conventional tests have not yet been developed. To oppose legislative discretion by undefined judicial standards of reasonableness is to oppose legislative by judicial discretion."

tion, and that explanation, it is suggested, is to be found on a relatively higher level of operation than that of being a substantive standard. For the conception of reasonableness has as a primary content a method and an attitude, which attitude is the teleological approach. It is a way of referring, not a content referred to. By an appeal to reasonableness, one cannot go to reasonableness and thereby determine anything. The appeal to reasonableness is not the end of an inquiry but the beginning. It primarily states a problem and focuses attention.

COMMON GOOD AND PUBLIC POLICY

The recourse in law to "considerations of public policy" is a common event and occurs frequently in deliberation by courts. The rapid growth, for example, of a large special interest such as labor, which previously had been relatively unorganized when compared to the special interest group of employers and business men with which it is now in conflict, introduces conflicts which, fortunately for both, the court has been permitted to mediate in part.[11] The adjustment of the interests involved has not been easy, and because of its difficulty and newness and because of the importance of these interests, reference to the "public interest" is a constant practice. In what sense there is an important public or disinterested third party in this issue, or whether the apparent third party is only so in appearance, may be difficult to determine. At present it is a matter of opinion, and the answer depends more on one's social philosophy than on an appeal to fact. However this may be, the courts are in fact constantly referring beyond the immediate interests involved either to find some intelligible ground of unity between the groups or to

[11] As exemplified in the decisions in LANDIS, CASES ON LABOR LAW (1934); Commons *et al.*, HISTORY OF LABOUR IN THE UNITED STATES (1935-36).

evaluate the merits of claims and counterclaims in terms of all the values and consequences involved or, in some sense, to protect the interest of the whole or the public. This is the case for a large part of our law. "The whole body of common law is made up of compromises of conflicting individual interests in which we turn to some social interest, frequently under the name of public policy to determine the limits of a reasonable adjustment."[12]

This reference to the public interest and the common good and the circumstances under which appeal is made are readily apparent in labor law. It is a dominant reference in constitutional law where, for example, public policy is an alternative wedge to reasonableness in determining due process and where police power to regulate for the general welfare competes with due process for the approval of the courts in constitutional questions concerning legislation.[13] Yet while it is accepted doctrine in American constitutional law that the doctrine of police power is a controlling principle, limited only by a standard of proper exercise both with respect to ends and means which are in turn estimated by the standards of reasonableness and the "due process of law" clause,[14] it is an equally accepted criticism of constitutional law that the police power clause is what the courts say it is, or, in other words, is basically an elastic, indeterminate instrument of decision. That decisions validating and nullifying legislation are made in terms of this concept is apparent, but the grounds of such discrimination respecting legislation must be looked for beyond the doctrine itself. "It defies legal definition—as a response to the dynamical

[12] Pound, *A Theory of Social Interests* (1921) 15 PAPERS AND PROCEEDINGS OF THE AMERICAN SOCIOLOGICAL SOCIETY 16, 17.

[13] WILLIS, CONSTITUTIONAL LAWS (1938).

[14] FREUND, POLICE POWER, PUBLIC POLICY AND CONSTITUTIONAL LAW (1904)

aspects of society, it cannot be reduced to a constitutional formula."[15]

Its elasticity is indicated in the attempts of courts to define it.

> Police power is the name given to that inherent sovereignty which it is the right and duty of the government or its agents to exercise whenever public policy in the broad sense demands, for the benefit of society at large, regulations to guard its morals, safety, health, in order to insure in any respect such economic conditions as an advancing civilization of a highly complex character requires.[16]

Its expansive and indeterminate character and range have been fortified by identifying it with immutable principles,[17] and today there is hardly a phase of law which is not affected by either the constitutional formula of police power or the wider conceptions of public policy and general welfare. The moral philosopher will recognize here at once, even as judges have from time to time, the ideal of the common good which is at the heart of so many of our philosophical formulations of social values.[18]

[15] Frankfurter, *Police Power* in ENCYCLOPEDIA OF THE SOCIAL SCIENCES.

[16] Eakin in Stetler v. O'Hara, 69 Ore. 519, 531 (1914).

[17] *Ibid.*, 532: "There have been many attempts to define the police power and its scope; but because of confusing the power itself with the changing conditions calling for its application many of the definitions are inexact and unsatisfactory. . . . The courts have latterly eliminated much of this confusion by pointing out that instead of the police power being expanded to meet new conditions, the new conditions are, as they arise, brought within the immutable and unchanging principles underlying the power."

[18] "The object and end of all government is to promote the happiness and prosperity of the community by which it was established; and it can never be assumed that the government intended to diminish its power of accomplishing the end for which it was created." Chief Justice Taney in the Charles River Bridge case, 11 Pet. 420 (1837). Quoted in CORWIN, THE TWILIGHT OF THE SUPREME COURT (1934) 65. See also Corwin's (*Ibid.*, 65 ff.) interpretation of the history of the conception of police power with its beginning in an attempt to meet the issue of vested rights early in our constitutional law controversies and with its subsequent periods of strength and weakness in the course of public events.

The explicit impact of considerations of public interest upon specific legal processes is, it should be remembered, an impact and a cutting in upon other considerations and procedures. An illustration of this is Justice Cardozo's statement in a case involving the determination of the responsibility of a parent corporation for liabilities incurred by a subsidiary: "The logical consistency of a juridical conception will indeed be sacrificed at times when the sacrifice is essential to the end that some public policy may be defended or upheld."[19]

The conception of the common good includes as full a range of values as does reasonableness, though focus and emphasis in each are different. Like "reasonableness," it has a native indeterminateness, and, at the same time, it comprises a multiplicity of values, some of which do and others of which do not hang together. "Public policy" gets its specific meaning from the context in which it is made relevant, but no one meaning or integrated system of meanings exhausts its application. That it is used to mean a preference of many individuals' interest to the immediate interest of a particular individual gives it a special focus. But this does not imply either that the "public" is something over and above all the interested members or that it may not be used to justify the preference of a special interest which all do not share. For it is used with both emphases. The inclusion in one formula of the common good with interests which are, in the ordinary course of affairs, considered as primarily personal is, in particular instances, an incompatible mixture. Nevertheless, it is typical of general formulae which are the legal exemplifications of principles of justice that they express potentially incompatible emphases, and, moreover, from any one emphasis a pathway within the formula is to be found to the others.

[19] Berkey v. Third Avenue Railway Co., 244 N.Y. 84 (1926).

This is illustrated in the manner in which public officials might have incorporated child labor laws within the area of Federal jurisdiction. The powers implicitly given the Federal government to make regulations in the interest of the general welfare was a conception sufficiently elastic for use to justify child labor laws on the ground of the national interest in a strong potential war reserve. The interest of an underprivileged group in health and leisure becomes an interest of the whole group in its fighting strength.[20] This type of interrelation between divergent interests has many other illustrations. The long fight to maintain the doctrine of freedom to contract was in part fought within the limits of the formulae of public policy, and both types of interpretation of public policy were taken in defense of this vested interest. On the one hand, the courts asserted that public policy operates to render void only those contracts which affect all society, while, on the other hand, it was argued that full freedom of individual action is the one preeminent attitude public policy requires.[21] The weakness of the present-day ideal of public policy as exhibited by the common law, it has been ably argued, is that "it is too exclusively to the advantage of the many and not sufficiently a regard for the claims of individual personality."[22]

THE CHARACTER OF DUE PROCESS

While such principles as the reasonable and public policy have a fairly clear reference to fundamental ideas

[20] Literally speaking, the Federal government is not empowered to pass laws merely because they are for the general welfare. The net effect, however, of its power to tax for the general welfare, plus its power to regulate interstate commerce, to declare war, and its powers under the police power clause is to make the statement substantially true.

[21] FREUND, STANDARDS OF AMERICAN LEGISLATION (1917) 54, 55, and cases cited there.

[22] *Ibid.*, 51, 70. See also GOODNOW, SOCIAL REFORM AND THE CONSTITUTION (1911) 329 ff.

and while the Constitution of the United States is now held to lay down the fundamental principles of just government, the earlier decisions of the United States Supreme Court on important issues turned to the traditional expressions of natural law doctrine for their support.[23] Thus, in the famous case of *Calder v. Bull,* Judge Chase writes:

> There are certain vital principles in our free republican governments which will determine and overrule an apparent and flagrant abuse of legislative power. . . . An act of the legislature contrary to the first great principles of the social compact cannot be considered a rightful exercise of legislative authority.[24]

Even more definite is Mason in *White v. White:*

> The security of the citizen against such arbitrary legislation rests upon the broader and more solid ground of natural rights and is not wholly dependent upon these negatives upon the legislative power contained in the constitution . . . the exercise of such a power is incompatible with the nature and object of all government.[25]

By 1890 the due process clause had assumed the role of the high standard of justice.[26] "It may be admitted that the words 'due process of law' as used in the 14th Amendment protect fundamental rights."[27] The language of Andrews in *Bertholf v. O'Reilly* clearly recognizes the shift that has been made from the "law behind the law" to the written Constitution:

[23] See Corwin, *The "Higher Law" Background in American Constitutional Law* (1929) 42 HARVARD LAW REVIEW 365; Haines, *The Law of Nature in State and Federal Decisions* (1916) 25 YALE LAW JOURNAL 617; Harper, *Natural Law in American Constitutional Theory* (1927) 26 MICHIGAN LAW REVIEW 62.

[24] 3 Dall 386, 388 (1798). See also Wilkinson v. Leland, 27 U.S. 627, 657 (1829); Fletcher v. Peck, 6 Cranch 87 (1810); Terrett v. Taylor, 9 Cranch 43, 49 (1815).

[25] 5 Barb. 474, 484, 485 (N.Y. 1849).

[26] HAINES, THE REVIVAL OF NATURAL LAW CONCEPTS (1930).

[27] Howard v. Kentucky, 200 U.S. 164, 173 (1906).

under the broad and liberal interpretation now given to constitutional guarantees, there can be no fundamental rights which will not fall within express or implied prohibitions and restraints of the Constitution, and it is unnecessary to seek for principles outside of the Constitution, under which such legislation may be condemned.[28]

Justice Field in his dissenting opinion in the *Slaughter House Cases* heralded the identification of natural rights and due process.[29] He said:

The 14th Amendment secures the like protection of all citizens. . . . That amendment was intended to give practical effect to the declaration of 1776 of inalienable rights, rights which are the gift of the creator, which the law does not confer but only recognizes.[30]

Later this attitude became the official attitude of the court when Justice Field wrote the majority opinion for a similar case.[31] The decline of the free appeal to natural law is met by the extension of the due process clause to take its place. "One might well style the type [of natural law] which has been most in evidence in American decision a political natural law . . . and the phrase 'due process of law' has been construed to be declarative thereof."[32] Originally a particular rule regulating procedure, it has become, especially since its inclusion in the 14th Amendment, an inclusive formula and symbol for justice.[33]

[28] 74 N.Y. 509, 515 (1874).

[29] 16 Wallace 36 (U.S. 1873).

[30] *Ibid.*, 105.

[31] Butchers' Union Slaughterhouse and Livestock Landing Co. v. Crescent City Co., 111 U.S. 746 (1883).

[32] Pound, *The Ideal Element in American Judicial Decision* (1931) 45 HARVARD LAW REVIEW 136. See Winfield, *Ethics in English Case Law* (1931) 45 HARVARD LAW REVIEW 112; HAINES, THE REVIVAL OF NATURAL LAW CONCEPTS (1930) 104–33; WRIGHT, AMERICAN INTERPRETATIONS OF NATURAL LAW (1931).

[33] See CORWIN, THE TWILIGHT OF THE SUPREME COURT (1934) Chapter II. In one sense it has been a negative symbol for justice, for its use has been largely to call actions into question. It is therefore unlike the conceptions of police power and general welfare which are positive justifica-

The due process clause has indubitably had a fundamental role in American judicial opinions. It has been a "basis" for decisions in an ever-widening number of disputes brought before the courts.[34] Even if its intimate relations to natural law formulae were not appreciated, its scope would be sufficient evidence of its affinity to those expressions which traditionally have been the bearers of the fundamental meanings of justice.[35] In an era when radical changes are made specific through legislative and administrative acts, the formula which purports to measure the legitimacy of those acts will have a wide range of application.

In estimating the role of the due process clause as a standard that directs specifically, two factors must be taken into account. In the first place, the due process clause has an initial meaning of its own in that it operated originally as a standard for criticizing the procedural aspects of official action. It is only comparatively late in its history that it has been used as a standard for criticizing substantive law. As a measure of whether an act was in accordance with "the law of the land" it had enough specificity to direct criticism in determinate directions. In the second place, and more important, in its use as a standard for judging substantive law it has come

---

tions of the acts of the state and federal governments. In another sense, however, it is equally positive with these other standards. For to assert that an act does not take away life, liberty, or property without due process is itself a legitimation of the act.

[34] For discussion of the type of extension given to the due process clause, see Pound, *Liberty of Contract* (1914) 23 YALE LAW JOURNAL 472 ff.; DICKINSON, ADMINISTRATIVE JUSTICE AND THE SUPREMACY OF LAW IN THE UNITED STATES (1927) Chapter VI; Hale, *Rate Making and the Revision of the Property Concept* (1922) 22 COLUMBIA LAW REVIEW 209; Hamilton, *The Path of Due Process of Law* in THE CONSTITUTION RECONSIDERED (1938) 167–91.

[35] HAINES, THE REVIVAL OF NATURAL LAW CONCEPTS (1930) 230: "The moral obligation to govern reasonably and justly was translated into legal phraseology by means of the old common law precept—due process of law."

to embody, in the form of precedent, a sizable quantity of principles, more or less stable, governing a variety of subject matters, which principles, in the course of constant application, have acquired specific content. These principles and decisions judges, particularly in the lower court, hesitate to disturb. In these respects there is little question but that the due process clause, taken as a collective concept, helps to guide decision.[36] As a procedural check upon acts of officials, due process is, however, only a partial answer to the problem of the role and the character of an inclusive expression of justice; so also are the decisions which are determined in the light of previous specific decisions of the due process clause. To treat them otherwise is to assume that the precedents now part of the meaning of the due process clause were themselves derived from the due process clause operating as a determinate standard.

It is in the operation of the due process clause in cases involving relatively unprecedented matters and those involving questions of broad social policy that its character is best revealed. Significantly, however, it is precisely in these situations that in order to predict or to evaluate one must go beyond the clause. The outcome of disputed cases has depended upon the economic, political, and social perspectives of the members of the court, together with the pressure of public opinion upon those members.[37] The clause itself can tell us very little. "At no place has free decision been more frequently called into service than in the interpretation of due process of law."[38]

[36] See LEWIS, A HISTORY OF AMERICAN POLITICAL THOUGHT (1937) 109–16.

[37] COMMONS, THE LEGAL FOUNDATIONS OF CAPITALISM (1924); CORWIN, THE TWILIGHT OF THE SUPREME COURT (1934); Cushman, *The Social and Economic Interpretation of the Fourteenth Amendment* (1923) 20 MICHIGAN LAW REVIEW 737; HAINES, THE REVIVAL OF NATURAL LAW CONCEPTS (1930) 122–43, 145–49, 196–212, 230–31; WARREN, THE SUPREME COURT IN UNITED STATES HISTORY (1935) 19 ff.

[38] HAINES, THE REVIVAL OF NATURAL LAW CONCEPTS (1930) 329.

In its operation, and by virtue of its extension and elasticity, the due process of law clause means ultimately "the approval of the court."[39] One cannot account for actual decisions on the basis of the due process clause alone.[40] The point is not that the due process clause is useless except as a device.[41] The question is whether it is possible to use it both as a generic expression of the basic standards of law and at the same time and in the same sense as a determinate guide in making evaluative judgments.

While the due process clause has been the legal battlefield of most of the important political, economic, and social issues, it is significant that the clause was not inevitably the scene of these controversies and was ill-adapted in many ways to a clear presentation and argumentation of the broad issues that the court considered. Its applicability was hardly general enough to be the "standard" needed, and it is well known that the first bid for this role in law after the Civil War was the "privileges and immunities" clause, while the "equal protection of the laws" clause has in fact shared the burden with the due process clause. It was only through a series of paradoxes that the due process clause became a fundamental phrase in constitutional law.[42]

The answer to the question of whether the due process clause has indeed been a guiding standard for the decision of these large issues has been on the part of

[39] CORWIN, THE TWILIGHT OF THE SUPREME COURT (1934) 89. See HAINES, THE REVIVAL OF NATURAL LAW CONCEPTS (1930) 323–31; Commager, *Constitutional History and the Higher Law* in THE CONSTITUTION RECONSIDERED (1938) 225–44.

[40] Cohen, *Transcendental Nonsense and the Functional Approach* (1935) 35 COLUMBIA LAW REVIEW 809, 814 ff.; COMMONS, THE LEGAL FOUNDATIONS OF CAPITALISM (1924) 341 ff.

[41] Borgnis v. Falk, 147 Wis. 327 (1911), vividly illustrates the pliability of due process when it is treated as a device.

[42] Hamilton, *The Path of Due Process of Law* in THE CONSTITUTION RECONSIDERED (1938) 167–91.

most critical writers an unequivocal "no." True, the concept is sufficiently elastic to include these issues within the proper scope of adjudication. It has been under some circumstances, on the basis of an interpretation sufficiently narrow, adequate to exclude certain solutions to these issues. But in the former case, as an elastic criterion of inclusion, it was not a standard, and in the latter case it operated as a special rule or principle not equivalent to, or comparable with, a general formula of justice.

FUNCTIONS OF THE INDETERMINATE

The previous paragraphs have summarized some of the conclusions of legal scholarship concerning a few of our formulae of justice and have restated the senses in which they do not operate as standards. It is necessary to remember this, just as it is necessary to remember the nature of the judicial process in any final conclusion to which one may arrive concerning the idea of justice. It is necessary to remember that the closest operative analogues of the general idea of justice, the nearest equivalents of philosophical formulations of justice to be found in law, do not operate as the scales but as the contexts for weighing social issues. Nevertheless, these formulae in their elastic range clearly have functions in the legal process, and no amount of debunking should entirely obscure their value. A recognition of their legal and social uses helps to clarify the power and the limitations of a general idea of justice.

A general formula of justice is a category, the most obvious use of which is to enlarge the immediately apparent scope of specific causes or interests. To the extent that any particular interest is identified with justice, to that extent the appeal is widened beyond those persons directly affected. To succeed in identifying a claim with justice is to organize and to enlist sympathy on its behalf and, sooner or later, to gain recognition for it in the law court by virtue of the fact that the interest is wide enough to involve the whole community.[43] It becomes a "public" interest. If a person's interest in getting out of prison does not involve a question of "justice" that interest is at best the concern of his family and friends. But if, as in the Mooney case, justice is an issue, then the interest in Mooney's freedom becomes a public interest. The formula used may vary. In Mooney's case the conception of justice might take the form of "protection of the innocent." With child labor and its evils, the interest group is wider, yet it involves only a special interest. If the interest in abolishing child labor becomes the interest of the working class, a stronger pressure group is called into action, and if it is identified with justice, the whole community pressure is potentially brought to bear on the social inertia which permits children to work. Those who oppose such pressures are likewise forced to appeal not to the interest of employers, for that enlists only a small group, but to some formula of justice. Consequently, the opposition appeal is, perhaps, to the constitutional rights of the citizen. The fight is, in a sense, for the exclusive use of the label "justice." Both sides appeal to conceptions of justice which apart from this particular conflict are rationally integrated. To succeed in making one formula of justice dominant is not necessarily to establish its intrinsic superiority over another but more probably denotes the success of the special interest with which the formula is identified.[44]

The indefinite elasticity of the conception of justice, as embodied in legal formulae, provides a convenient instrument in the judicial process both for growth and for the limitation of change. Vinogradoff calls attention to

[43] See ROBINSON, LAW AND THE LAWYERS (1935) 218–19.

[44] CORWIN, THE TWILIGHT OF THE SUPREME COURT (1934) Chapter I.

the vital significance of general formulae of justice in operating as an instrument for fundamental change. An appeal to justice in the form of an appeal to natural law, he writes,

> is an appeal from Caesar to a better informed Caesar. It is an appeal by society at large . . . not against single decisions or rules, but against entire systems of positive law. Legislators are called in to amend law by separate statutes; judges may do a great deal in amending the law by decisions in individual cases, but the wisdom of legislators and equity of judges are by themselves powerless against systems, because they start from the recognition of the authority of positive law in general. And yet law, being a human institution, ages not only in its single rules and doctrines, but in its national and historical setting, and the call for purification and reform may become more and more pressing with every generation. Public opinion then turns from reality to ideals. Of course these conceptions of justice are themselves historical, but they are drawn not from the complicated compromises of positive law but from the simpler and more scientific teaching of philosophical doctrine.[45]

Because of their elasticity, these general formulae of justice are used time and again to unify and organize a full consideration of values and consequences. An appeal to them permits deliberation to survey the minutest and the most extensive effects of a judgment or a proposed course of action.[46] In the form of an appeal to the "reasonable," the reëvaluation of important and long-standing procedures and values in law in terms of their social relevance is possible. It permits evaluation of particular actions in terms of the small day-to-day variations which

[45] COMMON SENSE IN LAW (1914) 244, 245.

[46] It is notable that Williston argues for the need of principles in law not because it gives certainty but because it gives flexibility and opportunity for adapting law to social change. See his *Change in Law* (1935) 69 UNITED STATES LAW REVIEW 237, 240, and SOME MODERN TENDENCIES IN THE LAW (1929).

we label circumstances, and it permits modification of specific rigorous rules of formal law.[47]

As an instrument, a generic formula of justice is used to bridge the change from the established to the new. Every socially significant interest which seeks to achieve legal significance finds a convenient entrance through the portals of justice and its variant expressions. Standing with one foot in the realm of the legally recognized and with the other in an undefined realm that includes both utopian ideals and incipient social practices, formulae of justice enable practices, which grow up independently of and away from the formulated practices by which courts seek to adjust conflicts, to have their eventual day in court. "If we examine the law from antiquity to our own day we always find some category prepared to receive the new principles and we always find some phraseology that makes the category more acceptable to the legal mind."[48] On the other hand, it should be recognized that because justice is rooted in the legally established, it is used as well to defend inroads upon the *status quo*, possessing, as a particular right does, a prestige acquired by its long-standing identification with justice.[49] The prejudice, for example, which prevents long-needed changes in both civil and criminal procedure, such as restriction of jury trials and limitations on witnesses in the presentation of evidence, is in part a reflection of this.[50]

As a bridge, justice is useful in affording a continuous support for change, for while the ends and techniques of

[47] Pound, *The Theory of Judicial Decision* (1923) 36 HARVARD LAW REVIEW 808.

[48] ROBINSON, LAW AND THE LAWYERS (1935) 219. POUND, LAW AND MORALS (1926), treats this phase of the matter extensively under the conception of introducing ethical concepts into the law. See Cohen, *Jus Naturale Redivivum* (1926) 25 PHILOSOPHICAL REVIEW 761, 762; VINOGRADOFF, COMMON SENSE IN LAW (1914) 235 ff.

[49] See LASKI, GRAMMAR OF POLITICS (1925) Chapters II–III; ROBINSON, LAW AND THE LAWYERS (1935) 220.

[50] See, for example, HAGERTY, TWENTIETH CENTURY CRIME—EIGHTEENTH CENTURY METHODS OF CONTROL (1934).

law change, justice still "unifies" the whole and thus keeps law the "same." It enables the layman to keep his faith in the law and the lawyer to maintain his faith in the continuity of the tradition. This is important both to the layman and to the lawyer; at any rate, the persistent demand for continuity in change indicates with some probability that at least "layman's certainty," as distinguished from "lawyer's certainty,"[51] is an important consideration to be taken into account in judgment. An important legal or constitutional change is felt to be compatible with layman's certainty when it is identified with the continuum of moral ideas of the community.

> New interests seeking judicial recognition and judges recognizing such interests rarely are willing to admit that the interests are new. Such admission would fatally handicap what is always an attack upon old interests and conventional principles. . . . When the fathers set out to establish the rising interests of independent farmers and business men by means of a written constitution, they did everything they could to make the upstart interests look as venerable as possible.[52]

The use of a formula of justice lies in part in the support it gives to judgment in the face of ignorance and uncertainty. Scratch the situation where an appeal to the ends of law is made and one is likely to find uncertainty and ignorance as to just what is involved and how best to treat it.[53] Like the use of the jury to determine questions in such a way as not to embarrass future courts and future situations where the direction that ought to be taken has not made itself clear to the court,[54] formulae of justice

[51] The distinction is made by Cardozo (1932) 55 REPORTS OF NEW YORK STATE BAR ASSOCIATION 288.

[52] ROBINSON, LAW AND THE LAWYERS (1935) 219. ARNOLD, THE SYMBOLS OF GOVERNMENT (1935), makes this a central point in elaborating the "mysteries of jurisprudence."

[53] See CARDOZO, THE NATURE OF THE JUDICIAL PROCESS (1922) 131–32, 142–43.

[54] See ULMAN, A JUDGE TAKES THE STAND (1933).

are usable to "determine" decisions which involve matters about which one is not quite sure either as to direction or value.[55] To determine a case by using justice as a standard is to set no standard which later evaluation may not alter. When ultimate principles are appealed to, it is a sign that there is need for intelligence, vision, and investigation.

We have been concerned in this chapter to point out the essential elasticity and indeterminateness of the formulae of justice. Their elasticity resides in the fact that the range of values they are said to include, and, in consequence, the range of possible values they exclude, varies widely. The indeterminateness of the formulae is a concomitant of their elasticity and makes them particularly useful because their broader meanings lend themselves to the criticism of substantive standards. While their elasticity and indeterminateness render the general formulae in law useless for many direct functions, they yet have positive legal and social functions which derive especially from their basic characteristics. But elasticity and indeterminateness alone are not sufficient to account for their use and inevitable presence in legal discourse. Their relevance and power derive from the fact that they have meaning as general public expressions of justice, and it is because they are such that they have the characteristics they do. To the clarification of the phase of justice which they determinately represent, I shall turn in the last chapter. Meanwhile, it is necessary to consider, first, the conception of "legal justice" which, as a general formulation, has more definiteness than most of the others, and, second, the general character of formulations of justice in jurisprudence, particularly in this connection the conscious recognition and use of the elasticity of justice by legal realists.

[55] See GREEN, JUDGE AND JURY (1930).

CHAPTER IV

LEGAL JUSTICE

LEGAL JUSTICE, though used with legalistic precision to distinguish the technical from the generic conceptions of justice, is not an unambiguous conception, for in its definition terms are employed which themselves have long histories and many uses. It is to be distinguished from equity and grace on the one hand and social justice on the other. Tourtoulon delimits it when he says: "The law must be just even though justice is not good. Justice and good are not identical cases."[1] It is imaginatively expressed in these words: "Justice resides in Hell; in Heaven alone is mercy; on earth there is the cross." This is a conception which has played a long and sometimes bitter role in human affairs. Thomas Aquinas reconciles himself to the idea by filing its harsh edges at the cost of leaving almost nothing of the doctrine. Justice, it is argued, is obedience to law, but no law need be obeyed unless it is just in a "proper" sense. Such circumlocution either begs the question or destroys the distinction between legal justice and "proper"; in effect it denies the validity of the legal doctrine. But in so far as the doctrine is strictly held, it usually purports to impose on law a requirement of order, certainty, and, particularly, impartiality and equality in terms of which the others

[1] TOURTOULON, PHILOSOPHY IN THE DEVELOPMENT OF LAW (1922) Chapter XIV.

are frequently made relevant—in short the attributes of "strict" law. The peculiar locus of *jus strictum* is the courtroom and not the legislature, for it is the function of the judge to abide by the given law, to enforce the will of the sovereign lawmaker. To look for the consequences of his judgment is injustice in a judge who is asked to administer law and not policy. The idea does not necessarily deny the essentially instrumental function of judgment nor the fact that the subject matters of judgment are in substance extralegal; it necessarily asserts, however, that within the context of law, legal values and established legal norms must control that judgment and that the particular case must be treated as a case, not as an individual.

Such a position affords a convenient and illuminating attitude and context of values for considering, first, its limitations as a complete conception of the function of judgment; second, it offers an opportunity to illustrate the instrumental values of legal technique when attention is focused on the context of social processes; and, third, it affords an opportunity to deepen the emphasis upon the multiplicity and complexity of values in law in their relation to justice. The discussion of legal justice will be centered around two of these values, impartiality and equality.

IMPARTIALITY

As a collective concept, impartiality contains a group of specific values and interests which men treasure as safeguards against tyranny. It involves the interests of litigants in a "fair trial" and includes such factors as "judgment by one's peers," an opportunity for a "fair hearing," the elimination from judgment of the influence of personal relations and interests as between litigant and judge, such as friendship or financial ties.

Especially, it involves the interest in "equal" treatment, but since "equality" gives rise to its own special distortions when erected into a general definition of justice, explicit treatment of this aspect will be deferred.

An analysis of the limitations of impartiality, when impartiality is expanded to proportions which exhaust the meaning and use of justice, is not to be taken as a repudiation of the specific values of impartiality. On the contrary, it is to insist that they are specific values and are parts of justice only. To associate impartiality with the whole of justice leads to postulates which observation renders difficult to believe and necessitates the reassertion of doctrines which realists and others have seriously qualified; for example, the conception of antecedently given systems of laws or leading principles that could dictate their own special application with rigor and the conception of judgment as oracular and mechanical.[2] Law and impartiality so construed fail to reflect their own limitations and practical powers.

The insistence of realists on the limitations of impartial judgment has been frequently misunderstood. The import of their arguments has been taken to mean that judges are political opportunists. Though this is sometimes the case, it is not important to the argument. For in essence, the argument is not against particular acts of misjudging so much as it is an attempt to characterize the essential character of the best judge. Judges fail to be impartial not because they are vicious but because in the process of decision their sense of values is inevitably involved. Once it is recognized that laws are not dictators of decision but instruments of decision, the conception of impartiality must recognize its own limitations. We can-

[2] See Nelles, *Toward Legal Understanding* (1934) 34 COLUMBIA LAW REVIEW 862 ff.; Radin, *Permanent Problems of the Law* (1929) 15 CORNELL LAW QUARTERLY 1.

not then rest our idea of justice on impartiality where the latter is a concept of impartial deduction. Once we recognize that the heart of the problem of decision is the search for relevant premises, major and minor, impartiality is transformed into the search for the wise use of selected guides, not merely the formal use of given rules.[3] In short, the best that can be said of impartiality, if it is to be identified with the whole of justice, is that it means a sense of values influencing the judge which are acceptable to both parties, rather than strict impersonality, where "sense of values" means the wise use of legal and moral norms for clarifying and resolving conflict. Both the decisions and their principles must be tested at the very least by their ability to make peace, and in this sense all decisions are discovered to be policy-making acts. In such a situation, impartiality is reduced to an honest effort to do the best one can in reconciling apparently hostile consciences. This is certainly not impartiality in the old sense and, indeed, is hardly impartiality at all; it is something else, related to mediation. In still another respect, to identify justice with impartiality, once it is recognized that the fundamental legal postulates reflect a social frame of reference, itself developed in response to social and economic values, the conception of impartiality must be transformed from a disinterested application of antecedently given standards and systems to the publicly justifiable interest in significant consequences presented in particular disputes, the larger interests of which are supposed to be the judge's concern.[4]

The historical setting in moral theory for the doctrine

[3] CARDOZO, THE PARADOXES OF LEGAL SCIENCE (1928) 10: "So far as they [the judges] are the mere mouthpieces of a legislature . . . their activity is essentially administrative and not judicial. Where doubt enters in, there enters the judicial function."

[4] See Frank's vigorous statement of the limitations of strict impartiality. *Mr. Justice Holmes and Non-Euclidean Legal Thinking* (1932) 17 CORNELL LAW QUARTERLY 568, 578 ff.

of impartiality italicizes in its own way the difficulty attendant upon an excessive elaboration of the ideal of impartiality. Strict impartiality as a doctrine was fundamentally rooted in a conception either of natural law or of "disinterested benevolence" either in God or in man, in pure reason, or in self-evident truths and commands. Strict impartiality in judgment as an ideal was a corollary to these beliefs. But the difficulty in getting the moral law, thus established, persuasively into human operations soon led to the identification of the objective standard with an emotional and inner factor. In the case of Adam Smith, we arrive at the conception of the impartial spectator, and this meant disinterested benevolence or sympathy. But the identification of impartiality with interest and emotion is "the beginning of the end" of strict impartiality. Once this path is taken, one is led inevitably to a "moral sense." At such a point, one comes to eliminate impartiality altogether, or one revises what is meant by the term. Emotional impartiality is as close to a contradiction as one could wish in so far as impartiality is originally conceived as completely independent of individual interest. The error in the moral sense school was not in their premise, namely, that objective reason conceived either as natural law or the law of God has neither coercive authority over, nor practical use to, men unless it be somehow a part of their experience and interest; the error was in trying to establish universal judgment or strict impartiality at all. Such an enterprise illustrated the contradiction of human judgment and strict impartiality. In order to make strict impartiality workable it had to be denied by identifying it with some form of passion or impulse.

Those who have critically raised the question of the appropriateness of identifying impartiality with legal justice have not thereby sought to impugn its special function as a guide in the evaluation of legal acts. In so far as law is a matter of administration, impartiality as a standard is definitely pertinent to law. It is important but not exclusive. It comprises particular procedures governing the action of third parties.[5] As such it constitutes one group among others in the whole of justice. The attempt to limit the whole conception of justice to it fails basically on two counts. Impartiality is not, unless reinterpreted, pertinent where the problem of justice is the search for relevant ends and the adjustment of conflicting tendencies that law has come to recognize; and, even where pertinent, it is not exclusively controlling but is constantly qualified because of its harshness in actual practice. Justice is certainly not less than the actual practice of law.

In order to avoid misunderstanding, it needs reëmphasis that the premises and principles of legal realism do not imply the elimination of those values in so far as they are operative for any given classification of law. These values imply in general that within a given classification judgments are capable of criticism in terms of whether or not there has been an impartial and equal application of that classification to all parties who have rights or duties under that classification. To affirm the need for constant criticism of a classification with respect to its social adequacy is not to deny that any given classification ought to be faithfully administered. To criticize ex-

[5] Though usually associated with the procedural aspects of law in order to give impartiality determinateness, procedural law is distinguished from substantive law only relatively. Indeed some realists would go further and assert that, judged from the point of view of results, the distinction for many purposes becomes almost arbitrary. Arnold, in a review of Green's JUDGE AND JURY (1930) 40 YALE LAW REVIEW 833, said: "The difference between procedural and substantive law is a useful device for one who is making an index of decisions, but nothing more." See Cook, *Substance and Procedure in the Conflict of Laws* (1932) 42 YALE LAW REVIEW 358; Arnold, *The Role of Substantive Law and Procedure in the Legal Process* (1932) 45 HARVARD LAW REVIEW 617.

isting rules as not always in fact describing what rules and principles the courts actually operate with is not to deny that the actual rules should be faithfully adhered to. To insist that the value of any given decision must rest upon an evaluation of the consequences it effects is not to deny that faithfulness to uniform treatment is one of the values to be looked for and weighed. To insist that the classifications must be as socially relevant as possible and that, therefore, concreteness is as much an instrumental value in judgment as generality is not to deny that concrete classifications, and those that draw adequate distinctions, should be conscientiously used. To hold that rules will be used to manipulate situations does not mean that they must always be so used, nor does it mean that such use is always to be preferred to more obvious but less just applications. Finally, to recognize that the just decision is frequently an object of search among various kinds of impartiality, that rules are consequences of decisions as much as creators of decisions, is not to assert that law has no rules which may be impartially and equally administered and honestly used in analysis.

There are few theorists who defend the traditional theory of impartiality today. The entire rationalistic approach, of which the overemphasis upon impartiality is but one result, carries little weight in contemporary analysis. Nevertheless, the effects of the older attitude persist. Hence, while men may not defend impartiality as rationalistically construed, they yet espouse a notion of what might be termed "sporting justice." The new language has different overtones and is associated with new moral codes, especially that of sport. To conceive of law as the rules of a game and the judge as umpire is, however, merely a reformulation of the ideal. In some ways, this concept of "sport law" represents a peculiarly American adaptation of the doctrine of impartiality; and it is easy to understand how the analogy of a game would appeal to the American mind. Even in America sporting justice can not, however, be said to have achieved a complete juristic expression. It is rather to be found in the form of premises of arguments and in popular discussion of legal problems.[6] Judge Hobson's charge to the jury illustrates an application of the sport conception to the field lying between the procedural and the substantive parts of law:

> You men are like an umpire at a ball game; you are in a position to see the pitcher and how he throws the ball. If it comes in above the knees and below the shoulder, fairly well over the plate, call it a strike. If it is above the shoulder or below the knees, call it a ball. It must be one or the other. Don't favor the home team and don't favor the visiting team. Give them all an even break. Apply the same principles an umpire at a ball game applies, in deciding the issue before you. You have a right to use your common sense and your own experience in life in arriving at the truth. That is all we want here.[7]

Social conflicts are now regarded as analogous to athletic contests. The marble lady with the blindfold, who is unable even to see the somewhat antiquated balances she uses to weigh imponderables, is replaced by the alert

[6] See, for example, *Law and Fair Play*, 5 FORTNIGHTLY LAW JOURNAL 39; *Justice, a Game* (1928) 31 LAW NOTES 186; *Lopsided Justice*, an editorial in the New York Times, October 24, 1938; an address by Associate Justice McReynolds, reported in the New York Times, March 16, 1937: "We must choose between a government that acts as umpire and one which interferes in the lives of its citizens taking sides"; a radio address by Representative Dies, September 17, 1939. See also Pound, *Do We Need a Philosophy of Law?* (1905) 5 COLUMBIA LAW REVIEW 339, 347. Wigmore has shown time and again how the sportsman's theory of justice permeates the common law rules of evidence and procedure. See WIGMORE, EVIDENCE (3d ed. 1940) Sections 57 (character rule), 1845 (discovery), 2251 (privilege against self-incrimination).

[7] Reported in the New York Times, August 24, 1937. It should be noted that strictly speaking "common sense and your own experience in life" have no place in the baseball rule book. The analogy breaks down.

man in white with a whistle, by the unpopular gentleman in black who rules the baseball diamond, or by the expert observer on the sidelines. If the legal machinery is now forced to operate from the umpire's stand instead of from the confines of the inner temple, it is because the subject matter as conceived has changed in essentials. The idea of competition comes to be more a fundamental attitude than that of "promise-performance."[8] Whereas impartial blind justice was only in a sense adaptable to the idea of competition, "sporting justice" is harmonious with it. Justice as "sporting fairness" appears to be acceptable today because it is apposite to the present situation, while impartiality of the "blind" type is evidently antique.

Given the fact of competition, the conception of "sporting justice" attempts to understand law as the rules of competition, dictated by the needs of competition. Such being the case, its principle becomes that of "fairness," but "fairness" is not to be identified with a transcendental "ought" nor with a "harmony" of decisions with universal principles. This notion of "fairness" involves as much of equity as of *jus strictum.* This conception needs no theories of subjection, social contract, or government to enable either the players or the umpire to understand the rules imposed on both. The ideal of conduct is embodied in the ideal of sportsmanship. One takes one's losses and begins again; raw decisions are taken for what they are, with complaint but without rebellion. The game is a good game when the sides are well matched and the interest is great. The function of rules

[8] The conception of impartiality antedates, of course, the rise of our economy, and its ideological superstructure and the fact of competition is as old as society. Impartiality was, however, easily adaptable to the special needs of the modern system of free competition with its concomitant demands that governmental interference be the exception rather than the rule. The refusal of the courts to give declaratory judgments is but one phase of this general picture.

is to govern neither little nor much but to judge well—that is, to enforce the rules of competition precisely.

Given the fact of competition and the conception of the game, formulae like *suum cuique tribuere* lose the controlling significance they were supposed to have either as a rationale or as an instrument of decision. For, once it is recognized that "ownness" is a creature of the game, the formulae of property assume a secondary significance, determined as they are by the competition itself. Rights and duties are not so much creatures of law as the laws themselves from the player's point of view. The same context evades most of what is considered central in orthodox formulations of the principles of legal justice; but the sportsman idea is not in contradiction with the correlative economic framework of legal justice nor with the possible rationale of that framework. The same may be said of the notion of "each according to his merit" as a principle of legal justice, but with this difference, that merit is not question begging in its athletic sense. In the economic framework, merit is identical with bargaining power. The problem of legal justice thus becomes not that of giving according to merit but rather that of determining merits by what can be gotten "fairly."

Coincident with this freedom to play the game is another, namely, a release from any necessary alliances with the conception of law as command. For, with competition as central, the command character of law becomes incidental in the total complex of the game. Naturally, there is no need to deny the compulsory character or sovereignty of umpire law nor the fact of the dependence of ultimate practical responsibility on some institution or person for revising the laws from time to time. What is denied is that there are any interests beyond the players. For such a theory the sovereign has no will, as he has for an analytic jurisprudence with all the implications of positive government. And, on the other hand, justice so conceived is not of necessity tied up with the notions of the historical school (except in the sense that the rules of the game are in part historically given), nor with those of the evolutionary school (though survival of the fittest may furnish a rationale for this theory),[9] nor with the legal metaphysicians, nor yet even with the "consent of the governed" and social contract school of jurisprudence, although to the latter it has a close relation. Yet even in this case, the sporting principle of law may escape one of the chief criticisms urged against the contract notion, that a contract implies a legal context to begin with, for the sporting theory is not concerned with historic or postulational justification of the procedures of the game. Law from this perspective is a work of artistic creation, a refinement of a more basic social process, constructed not in its own interests but to enhance economic interests. The primacy of the social, even the economic, is not taken for granted.

From one point of view the shift to a competitive rationale of law is a shift from the position of protecting what individuals have acquired through competition to the conception of protecting competition. Even a Marxian analysis might grant that this is one way of expressing the compromises the ruling class has made with the forces of labor, and there is little doubt that this does in fact describe much that has happened in the last half century.

[9] It is convenient to point out here the distinction existing between this sporting theory and the biological theory of competition or struggle. Whereas Spencer, for example, builds a rationale out of the materials of a hastily understood evolutionary biologism, competitive law finds its implication and limits within the social milieu, and whereas Spencer is concerned to find generic laws rooted in biology which shall apply as genus to species to the field of human acts and regulation, the notion of competition makes no such facile elaborations. Because one chooses to take competition as central, it by no means implies that one has found the equivalent on the social plane for what is a struggle for the survival of the fittest in the plant and animal world.

One calls to mind the attempted limitations of monopoly or in recent times the partial attacks on holding companies. In this sense, Brandeis is the archapostle of this point of view.[10] Laws to protect the middle class have occupied a good deal of the attention of the courts and the legislatures. The attempt to maintain the equality of bargaining power between individual and individual, group and group, and class and class has been repeated in almost every capitalistic country in the world.[11]

The conception of sporting justice might have had a longer life had it received its formulation when the economics of competition received its formulation. It might then have become a tradition with a vested interest. The weakness of the theory today is, however, apparent. The game has become too brutal, too destructive of human life, too exhaustive to those who win, and too fatal for those who lose. Living begins to look more like a struggle than a game. The participant's sense of humor and sense of balance are worn, and the sporting morale is breaking up into a fighting morale. The sides are too unequal for successful competition, and, in the eyes of the defeated, the game looks more like exploitation than competition.

Another fact today makes the umpire theory seem antiquated, namely, the extension of the powers and activity of government. The government has with increasing impetus extended its creative functions and is, almost as much as anything else, a player in the game.[12] In short, the power and profession of settling conflicts, which is a business among other businesses,[13] are now only part of

[10] See, for example, Brandeis, Other People's Money (rev. ed., 1932). See also Mason, Brandeis (1933) 64.

[11] Frank, Save America First (1938) Chapter II.

[12] See Frankfurter, The Public and Its Government (1930) Chapter II.

[13] It may be noted in passing that like any other business its ultimate success depends upon satisfying the customers and, as Spinoza long ago pointed out, failure to do so in the long run means disaster.

"government." Government, not content with adjudicating disputes after they have arisen, has gone increasingly into the business of administering "public" affairs, goods, and interests, sometimes frankly in competition with private concerns. In avoiding the incidence of disputes, it has increasingly taken over activities previously conducted by other groups, entering directly into the business of production and distribution. In general, government is increasingly becoming a creator and protector of a host of goods: health, social security, and many economic goods. In these circumstances, "justice" demands "fairness" to the umpire, and the whole idea begins to break down.

Strictly speaking, the umpire in a game need have no sympathy for the loser; his job is to make impartial judgments, and his interest is essentially in the competition itself. Sympathy is completely irrelevant and, if present, constitutes a serious threat to the impartiality of competition. Present-day government has found it both necessary and proper, however, to abandon umpire impartiality. Having acquired first a sensitivity to the fact that losers are beaten so badly, it has proceeded to balance the competition itself, and this comes in practice to mean a vital interest in helping the victim of competition. In short, the umpire becomes a person with his own interests and emotions, and it is humanly impossible for him merely to "observe." This is illustrated in the recent proposal of Senator O'Mahoney whose suggestion, typical of the trend, is that minority stockholders be represented by a governmental representative in meetings of large corporations. The god of wrath judging good and evil becomes a shepherd defending the sheep. When he finds that, if the game of life is to be, someone must keep the players from harm, "fairness" transcends the context of sport and becomes something else and the context transcended becomes useless. The essential limitations of sporting fairness derive from the fact that a particular historical set of needs and situations has proved, again, an inadequate basis for an eternal *Grenzbegriff*.[14] True enough, competition may be eternal, but the conception here considered rests upon the premise that competition will not degenerate into life-or-death struggle; as this idea vanishes as a fundamental fact, the theory necessarily loses its cogency—its reasons become fictions and distortions.

EQUALITY

We turn now to the discussion of the other aspect of legal justice, namely, equality. Equality and impartiality are rarely distinguished clearly. They are for the most part synonymous both in their emotional effects and in their denotations. The major difference is that impartiality attaches more especially to the person judging. Nevertheless, certain facts concerning the conception and the argument for legal justice, not brought out by considering impartiality, are clarified by reference to discussions which identify justice with equality. Legal equality is defined variously, but in its essential parts it amounts to this, that in the same circumstances, positively and negatively defined, all individuals are to receive the same treatment and that, roughly speaking, similar consequences are to attach to similar acts. Such a conception of equality, where it operates determinately within the limits thus defined, is a legitimate instrument of law used as much by necessity as by merit. It is a technical instrument and is one among many such legal procedures.

Criticism of the conception of legal equality is frequently made in terms of what is actually a substantive

[14] Freund, Standards of American Legislation (1917) 71: "The spirit of the common law was too neutral for an effective weapon against practices injurious to the weaker elements of society."

equality, of means, goods, opportunities, and the good life. It is this conception of equality that Bentham gives recognition to in his fourfold division of the ends of the civil code.[15] The criticisms of this notion made by Felix S. Cohen and others are well taken.[16] Equality involves selection and emphasis; though the term seems to emphasize an absence of essential bias, it can have no empirical meaning except as it isolates one interest to treat equally at the expense of others. To the general plea for equality, it is necessary to ask, "equality in what respect?" Equality involves a selection of data, which selection is normative and in need of justification. Very few situations are such that they need to be viewed only from one perspective. The basic criticism of equality, taken as the aim of law, is that it misleads, implying impartiality without qualification and, therefore, hiding the partialities of decision when otherwise construed. It is a confusing conception.

Such criticism is, however, irrelevant to equality in so far as equality is restricted to a collective group of specific procedural safeguards. If impossibility of performance voids a contract, then for any given individual the rule will hold when the circumstances such as are contemplated by the rule are present. Such a principle of uniform applicability may be invaded by changing the circumstances to which the rule is to be made generally applicable and by drawing exceptions for a particular case. This latter situation, individualization of judgment, includes at least three distinct types: (a) equity, (b) charity, or the recognition of the need for "favor," and (c) the unjust or procedurally unequal judgment. The difference between these three is not in the nature of the exceptions drawn but rather in the reasoning, the justifi-

[15] WORKS, edited by J. Bowring (1843) I, 302 ff.

[16] COHEN, ETHICAL SYSTEMS AND LEGAL IDEALS (1933) 77 ff.; see the introductory sections of HALE, LEGAL FACTORS IN ECONOMIC SOCIETY (2d. ed., 1937).

cation, and the content of the exception. In all three, the altered circumstances taken into account are not unique, though they may not be widely prevalent; they embrace, nonetheless, types of circumstances. Evils of the second and third order, to use Bentham's language,[17] are in operation, or are assumed to come into operation, with the inclusion of certain specific circumstances in the weighing of particular issues; when they are made to operate, we are aroused by the injustice of the judgment—there was no "equality before the law."[18]

What, in fact, constitutes the specific equalities of equal justice is a matter which depends both on investigation and evaluation. Even the matters excluded are not without possible qualifications. By taking advantage of the rule requiring a fair and full hearing, litigants frequently are able to defeat the purposes of justice by unique litigation involving delay, excessive expense, and the like. If limitations on a fair hearing in these circumstances are made, the question of their injustice is almost an academic matter.

An understanding of the value of equality is not helped much by transforming these values into illustrations of a general moral law of justice defined as the recognition of the "intrinsic equality of personality." "The equality of all men before the law is the juridical expression of the philosophical principle of the intrinsic equality of persons as persons."[19] Stace, in elaborating this conception, makes

[17] INTRODUCTION TO THE PRINCIPLES OF MORALS AND LEGISLATION (1927) 152.

[18] The issue is always present. Consider the conceptions of distribution of risk and liability without fault. Whether the financial ability to take a loss should have anything to do with the operation of rules governing liability is peculiarly interesting in view of the differences of opinion. Whatever their justification or lack of justification, the answers illustrate the fact that "equal treatment" involves more than an emotional response to "equality."

[19] STACE, THE CONCEPT OF MORALS (1937) 179. This approach, the transformation of justice and equality into a metaphysics of personality,

it clear that legal judgment has to do with "extrinsic" circumstances, that it takes account of extrinsic differences and upon them erects a basis for differences of treatment. Yet, if it does this, it is difficult to see why it does not base similarity of treatment upon extrinsic circumstances also. But if it does both, then the intrinsic equality of personality is empirically useless, since both substantive and procedural equalities are based on observable and objectively measured interests, claims, and values. To assert that equality of treatment does not need a justification, whereas unequal treatment does, is patently in opposition to the facts. At least in substantive equalities, law generally takes existing inequalities for granted, and equalities sought for need imperative justification for their recognition, since the introduction of any substantive equality usually involves shifts in existing distributions. The actual content of "equality before the law" is always justified or capable of being justified. The plain fact is that any determination may be called upon to justify itself.

The justification to be found for legal equality rests not so much on any value of personality as such, but rather the value directs attention to damages incurred by the law itself in the effective pursuit of its ends, generally expressed as the effective adjustment of conflict. In so far as the individual is made the center of this justification, part of it depends not on any intrinsic value of that individual but on his power. What Stace might have said is: so distribute goods that where differences between claimants are not significant, or where claims have equal merit, distributions should be equal. The usefulness of this formulation would depend upon the possibility of defining "significance" and "merit," neither of which involves

is characteristic of a type of thought which has a clear formulation in Kant. We select Stace because he explicitly identifies equality and justice. He is, however, only one of many, such as Husserl, Hocking, and Urban.

equality of personality. If this is true, any further criticism of this position depends upon a consideration of concrete policies with which we are not here immediately concerned.

The idea of intrinsic equality of personality aids little in any realistic analysis of situations or in any understanding of the normative actions or ideals of public institutions. In fact, to hold with Stace that equality shall be a criterion when, and only when, other "legitimate" factors which take precedence over the criterion of equality are absent is to make inequality synonymous with the arbitrary. The arbitrary is that which lacks reason; so is the inequality that is contrasted with intrinsic equality. Both are negative; the unjust is inequality without extrinsic differences, and the arbitrary is that which is without purpose. The question in both cases is fundamentally not what are the absolute rights but what hypotheses in respect to forthcoming results permit the determination in question. To find none is to call it unequal, arbitrary, unjust. The "intrinsic equality of personalities" is thus a poor expression for the realistic demand that actions be reasonable.

Legal equality relates in the first instance to method in law. The statement over the Supreme Court of the United States, "equal justice under law," either reads better than it knows or it indeed possesses a discerning conception of legal equality and discriminates more than most phrases of a similar character. For, if this statement means any more than "just justice under justice," it implies a distinction between justice and equality where equality is not a noun as in the phrase "equality and justice" but is an adjective modifying justice where justice is not taken as meaning law. Unless "equal" is something apart from justice and belongs in part to a different category like "red" in "the red rose," it must, however, be taken as a part of justice like "red" in "the red color." In such terms, equality takes its place as a method of law, though by no means an exclusive method.

As a method in law, it has both its value and its limitation. Its value stems from its use as an instrument of criticism of court actions. Its limitation derives from the fact that it only rarely operates as an exclusive instrument of criticism of a particular act. Its value stems from the fact that where there is a scarcity of available legal energy, uniform procedure is as much a necessity as a value.

> *Stare decisis* is usually the wise policy, because in most matters it is more important that the applicable rule of law be settled than that it be settled right. This is commonly true even where the error is a matter of serious concern.[20]

At the same time its limitation appears in the fact that it frequently is only an indecent justification of a mechanized habit of action, an excuse for the failure of judges to assume responsibility for intelligent judgment and an excuse for ignorance where knowledge is not at hand but must be sought.

To place it in the context of law and conflict, and the problematic situation, is to see its power as a general yet meaningful prescription, ideal, or tool of analysis considerably diminished. Its appeal comes in part from placing it either in the context of adjudication of reward and punishment or the context of quantitative exchange and barter. The typical picture to form itself in the mind when legal equality is considered is that of possession of goods—loss of goods, through fraud, negligence, or robbery—the appeal to law—the restoration of the goods to the owner. The presence of such situations is quantitatively of importance in the administration of law. Any

[20] Brandeis in Burnet v. Coronado Oil and Gas Co., 285 U.S. 393, 406 (1932), cited in ROBINSON, LAW AND THE LAWYERS (1935) 295.

person justifiably expects that when he finds himself in the position of suffering unjustified loss, the instruments of law will be available to him. But this, it should be remembered, is in fact an *administration* of law, and legal judgment is, insofar, irrelevant. The burden of judgment comes in establishing these categories, in terms of which the mechanism of law comes into operation. The judgment is essentially prior to the use of equality of application or it is concomitant with it only when equal justice is possibly unjust.

For the most part, judgment occurs in the middle of things. Only Adam began with no human judgments preceding him, and even he found himself in the middle of an affair before he judged. Legal judgment differs from personal decisions not only in attempting to deal with universals, classes, regarding individual conflicts merely as "cases," but also in attempting to build up settled habits of decision, culminating in an order with a high degree of precision and a large fund of ready-made analysis. In the absence of "persuasive" alternatives, the principle of *stare decisis* has a heavy presumption in its favor—a natural presumption, indeed, so strong that its discovery has led many writers to idealize the mechanization of the whole process of judging. On the whole, for a new idea to be adequately "persuasive," the contrast between the merits of the established and the proposed must be strong. Even apart from the "legal values" in a precedent, even where a consideration of alternative ideas is given in terms of the social content and consequences of each, legal judgment, in precisely the same manner in which any other judgment within a situation that demands immediate decision acts, operates through inertia and habit. It requires a strong magnetic field to draw the planet of judgment out of its legal orbit. Habit, in whatever form it appears, and particularly where it is deeply ingrained by virtue of being public and having a recorded articulation, operates extremely efficiently, willy-nilly, to override the novel and distinctive features of a situation, to make believe, as it were, that all the aspects of the problematic can be solved by prescriptions derived from previous cases. In practice, most cases are placed into kinds; the problem in each case is formulated into a stereotyped form so that one problem looks like another; consequently, the solution to the class problem is supposed to work for every member. This drive toward the universal is one of the fundamental mechanisms in the creation of the conception of law.

Habits, both in men and in nature, have their value as necessities and are in practice converted into laws; but these same factors operate not only as necessities but also as rights, for there is generated from this process of necessities what might be called normal expectations in law.[21] These considerations operate most clearly in a context of the conflict of values where the general character of the problem is the establishment of rights and duties. Reference to the past, conformity to the past, to the established, application of the formulated to the to-be-formed, even though in procrustean fashion, serves those aspects of our relations to others which depend upon expectations, predictions—not all expectations, but a number of the more immediately important ones such as life, freedom, property, terms which are here used to stand as classes, whose particular historical members are subject to much diversity. The expectation that previously established rules and laws will be utilized in public judgment plays a tremendous role in the life of any community. The legal machine fosters those values—not alone to be sure, for other institutions and processes likewise aid in the realiza-

[21] See Radin, *Permanent Problems of Law* (1929) 15 CORNELL LAW QUARTERLY 1, 12 ff.

tion of these values in particular cases, but it is one of the more important agencies.

As a value, legal justice has, in addition to the positive content indicated above, a service to perform which is essentially negative but which, nevertheless, is important for an understanding of the role of legal justice in the contact of law and society as a whole. The institution of a public agency for the purpose of achieving better solutions to conflict has its own unintended by-product, namely, the problem of controlling the machine which has been erected. Even at the cost of the better solution in many cases, the instrument must be restricted. Such has been the judgment of the effective groups in our society. To give law a free hand involves too great a danger that the instrument may be put to undesirable use; wherefore, we attempt to limit the operation of its personnel by controls known collectively as legal or judicial justice. No one conscious of the two-edged character of an instrument as powerful as law can doubt the importance of the procedural controls law has devised for itself. These instruments of control we fairly call elements of "legal" justice because they are instruments for the solution to problems to which law gives rise. These same factors in a different context, namely, as values sought apart from their career as brakes on law or instruments for evaluating the actions of the personnel of law, are properly "social." The feeling emerges easily enough that legal justice is peculiarly the contribution and end of law which it adds to the sum total of our values. It definitely is peculiar to law on the whole, but it is peculiar because it represents a tentative method of solution to problems for which the presence of law itself is to blame. Social maladjustments which give rise to the need of a better methodology in law have themselves arisen frequently from an undue emphasis upon the values of legal justice.

A system of law which orients its thinking around its own systemic criteria inevitably creates a gap between social needs and the law. The law becomes unrealistic in its treatment of its problems, and it does so because of a tendency to retain as absolutes older estimations and classifications in order better to defend the values of equality before the law and of impartial administration. This unbalanced relation between the importance of legal values and of all other values necessitates a reversal of emphasis and the consequent establishment of a new point of equilibrium. Hence, the insistence upon legal justice as a necessity and only secondarily a duty, as frequently an imposition rather than a right; hence, legal justice as one of a wide variety of clashing values and suggestive criteria; hence, legal justice as a brake upon the operation of a machine and not its accelerator; hence, a critical attitude toward assertions of both the possibility and the desirability of excessive certainty in law.

CHAPTER V

PHILOSOPHIC JUSTICE

FORMULAE of justice are, as we have seen, important to any adequate conception of justice. Most philosophies of law seek, however, a more inclusive unity even than that provided by the formulae most frequently appealed to in law. We turn now to a consideration of some of the approaches to this more inclusive unity.

THE SENSE OF JUSTICE

This unity has frequently been found in what writers call a "sense of justice." Illustrations of the use of this formulation abound. "Our judges have . . . woven into the national, that is, the political life of the community, that instinct of justice."[1] Cohen writes: "Indeed, the body of law could not maintain itself if it did not conform in large measure to the prevailing sense of justice."[2] Stone is able to define justice so that "An act is just if it conforms to the sentiment of fairness which is an attribute of the human mind even under the most primitive conditions."[3] Radin has repeatedly built upon the sense of justice:

[1] Jenks, *The Function of Law in Society* (1923) SOCIETY OF COMPARATIVE LEGISLATION AND INTERNATIONAL LAW, 3d Series, Vol. V, Part IV, p. 176.

[2] *Jus Naturale Redivivum* (1926) 25 PHILOSOPHICAL REVIEW 761.

[3] LAW AND ITS ADMINISTRATION (1924) 27. See COUDERT, CERTAINTY AND JUSTICE (1913) 56; KRABBE, THE MODERN IDEA OF THE STATE (1913)

advantage and suffering have nowhere in organized society . . . been treated as purely economic matters. Other factors have entered into it, social, spiritual, personal. Out of these factors there has been created a social emotion which we call a sense of justice.[4]

These expressions, if taken as more than a metaphorical mode of speaking, will not withstand criticism. Few of the individuals here cited would defend the conception if it were taken literally as a biological trait of man.[5] Moreover, considered as a social resultant of many forces, it cannot be successfully defended as a standard or as an instrument of judgment and criticism. It is, however, a convenient shorthand expression of the ubiquitous relevance of justice in human affairs. Its use makes the elasticity of the conception explicit in a way that no other approach does. In appealing to a sense of justice, the individual is bringing into play the standards and possible ends-in-view which are relevant to one particular situation but which may not be relevant to other situations. The sum total of what may be brought into the estimation of the just act or decision, and nothing less, constitutes the meaning, for most writers, of the sense of justice.

MODES OF PEACE

Another attempt, frequently made, to formulate the inclusive unity of justice is that which equates justice with peace. The purpose of law is said to be the preservation

---

Chapter III; MILL, UTILITARIANISM (1864) 38. See also Duguit, *Objective Law* (1921) 21 COLUMBIA LAW REVIEW 17, 30–31; quoted in HALL, READINGS IN JURISPRUDENCE (1938).

[4] *The Chancellor's Foot* (1935) 49 HARVARD LAW REVIEW 48. He also states: "It is a poor sort of realism or experimentalism which disregards this sentiment of justice." See especially his LAW AS LOGIC AND EXPERIENCE (1940) Chapter V.

[5] Hobbes's criticism (LEVIATHAN, Chapter XIII) of a literal conception of a "sense" is still relevant: "Justice and injustice are none of the faculties neither of the body, nor of the mind. If they were they might be in a man that was alone in the world, as well as his senses and passions."

of peace, the settlement of conflict.[6] Narrowly construed, peace is the cessation of conflict. When two men fight and any of the following results occur, we may say that peace reigns: when both stop fighting from exhaustion or both are killed; when one wins and the other is cowed into submission by the superior strength of the other; when one leaves the field of battle because the object of the fight is not considered sufficiently vital to fight longer for it; when a third person enters the conflict and eliminates both contestants, leaving himself the winner, or arbitrarily decides that one who is his friend deserves the object fought for and joins with that individual and by actual or potential show of strength effects the submission of the other—in all these cases, peace in a strict sense ensues. We recognize in these situations the Hobbesian state of nature, of the war of all against all. Experience is ready at hand to illustrate the fact that this picture of the settlement of conflict is not a mythical characterization either of private or public conduct. The difficulty, apparent to all, with peace in this narrow sense is its temporary and negative quality. It is temporary because it depends upon the accident of superior force that rules for the present moment. At any future moment it may break down and conflict may recur. The peculiar emphasis of this peace is negative—negative in the sense that its definition and meaning are in terms of the absence of conflict. The positive character of this peace is at best

[6] See, for example, CARVER, ESSAYS IN SOCIAL JUSTICE (1915) 3 ff. As a way of particularizing the end of law, the conception of peace has been extensively used, particularly by those who, like many realists, see the origin of specific legal processes in the effort to settle conflicts. Characteristic of the Hobbesian approach to government, it has been especially used since the appearance of the conception of Darwinian evolution, and it colors the language even of those who are not drowned by evolutionism as Spencer and Carver were. See LLEWELLYN, THE BRAMBLE BUSH (1930) 110 ff., 116 ff. See also MILLER, THE DATA OF JURISPRUDENCE (1903) 207, 208, 220–31.

accidental, organized as it is by elements which are themselves instruments of war.

Although this kind of peace is a contemporary fact, it is not the whole or even the greater part of what we ordinarily understand peace to be. Organized society has substituted legal order for direct conflict as the important instrument of peace. This substitution need not be, nor is it in fact, such a qualitative change as we are prone to believe. In its lowest terms, the legal order simply stands for the intervention of third parties into a conflict which formerly contained only two. Ordinarily, we would not consider this so much a reign of legal order as of political order. But the two are intimately connected. The Curia Regis of the thirteenth and fourteenth centuries was primarily an instrument of political domination.[7] A centralized court system meant centralized power, and it was the desire for centralized power as much as or more than the decline of baronial and church courts that led to the concomitant rise of the Curia Regis. It is, however, irrelevant whether in particular historical situations legal peace was instrumental to political power or whether the reverse was true. It suffices to recognize their interdependence. It is more important to recognize that peace is definitely extended by the presence of a political power sufficiently strong to dominate all other groups, whether that domination be for the benefit of a dominant group or for the benefit of several groups. This is true whether or not the political order is supplemented by a legal order. In countries like Italy, Germany, and Russia, the reign of law over men is today in many ways inferior as an instrument of peace to the dominance of men over law. It is a mistake to identify a desired result solely with one

[7] Holdworth, History of English Law (1927) Vol. II, Book III, Chapters I–V.

type of technique when experience points to many instruments that achieve the same end.

The peace that results from the operation of a political force differs from a primitive peace. In effect, political peace has made operative three factors which were only implicit in primitive peace—it has added one instrument, centralized power; one condition of peace, the inability of the individual to enter into physical conflict with that power; and one result, the spatiotemporal extension of peace. By virtue of this additional machinery, peace now has a new instrument and a new content. Its operation is this, that it creates peace by enjoining, or more positively by commanding, that certain relations shall be handled in such and such a way. If the ruled follow the rules, then conflict will not occur; if the rules are violated, then the court will proceed to settle the conflict that arises by deciding who is right, that is, who has stayed more closely to the commands of the sovereign. With this, peace comes to include a relative impartiality, equality, and uniformity.

The introduction of rules for preventing disputes and for deciding existing disputes may not be materially a great step forward. It signifies a small advance or change from mere centralized power. This is particularly true with the rule considered simply as a command. The command may be anything, either positive or negative; in either case its operation, in theory at least, is the same. Moreover, a rule may be a universal class containing but one member. The most arbitrary single decision by a prince is still a rule, though at this point it becomes identical with the operation of political peace. And, finally, the rule may be such that it draws the most unequal distinctions within the rule or may apply only to certain sections of the ruled; yet, for all this, it is a rule for avoiding and settling conflicts.

The further expansion of the concept of peace takes three main lines: (1) there is the more definite and controlled content given to the broader ideas of impartiality and equality; (2) there is the development of specific court mechanisms which become more widely available to the people; and (3) there is the development of the broader conception of rules to the point where rules are instruments of peace because they incorporate procedures which eliminate the causes of conflicts and do not merely regulate the operations of conflicts that have already occurred. It is at this point that a conception of peace comes to be a unified conception of the complete purpose of law. The subject matters of conflict are the goods and values that men seek, and an *ideal* peace is realized only if there exists an economy of abundance in which common and private well-being are achieved. From this point of view the overall problem of organized society is production and distribution. Construed in these terms, the ideal of peace reaches beyond the work of law and becomes the bearer of values whose realization involves the total effort of the whole community.

It is apparent from this analysis of peace that to equate justice with peace in its fullest sense is to identify justice with anything from the mere absence of conflict to a utopia. If we restrict the ends of law to achieving a limited peace, we do so only by fiat. For peace has a dialectic, both logically and in fact. Though it has a use when limited to its restricted meanings, peace is not justice but a particular value, and as such it is in conflict with other practical ends and in that sense with justice. In law, "justice is never as important as order," writes Llewellyn.[8] With equal cogency, it might have been said that peace in its limited sense as an objective of law is more what law seeks to realize than peace in its more ideal sense.

[8] THE BRAMBLE BUSH (1930) 110.

DECENCY

"Justice," says Llewellyn, "is the decent fulfillment of decent expectations—of decent hopes."[9] Now "decent expectations" might mean anything. It might include the widest realizations of law or only very limited purposes. Injustice might mean the failure or the violation of expectations regarding special business promises or regarding complete social ideals. A "decent hope" might be an expectation that "needs" be fulfilled, that "merit" be rewarded, or that prior commitments and obligations be satisfied. The decent expectation may be that the law stick to an elastic promise to work for the better, it may only be that the expectation is that the law remain faithful to ways of acting which have been imposed upon it from time to time or are imbedded in the tradition, or it may mean only what is reasonable under the circumstances. For Llewellyn, this manner of formulating the conception is to indicate roughly that not all hopes are realistically possible and that the kind of justice possible is a function of the social situation. This latter includes not only goods but procedures available. Because a complete conception of justice is utopian, Llewellyn wishes to emphasize the conception of justice as limited. "Justice operates under the principle of scarcity." But this is exactly what is intended by the statement that "justice is never as important as order." In short, though there may be ideal solutions to conflict, the scarcity of energy in law and of goods in society may make mere settling of the dispute the best that can be accomplished. Llewellyn is not so much setting a contrast between order and justice as he is establishing a distinction and indeed an opposition between different conceptions of "order" or different

[9] The quotations in this paragraph are taken from unpublished lectures given by Llewellyn at the New School for Social Research, New York, in 1938.

extensions of the meaning of justice. Justice is neither taken in its widest application nor in its narrowest. The "decent" is a qualification calling attention to the "practicable," on the one hand, and the "approved" or "justified," on the other. It indicates respect not for all interests or values but for some, and of those some, many are "practicable" and many are not. It is almost entirely a description of what law is trying to do, not a prescription of what it ought to do. It does not define an end or detail a standard. It does not state that either the fulfillments are consistent or that the expectations are unified. The whole normative problem of law may be said to be reconciliation of decent expectations with one another and with equally acceptable manners of fulfillment. The definition is for this purpose practically open at both ends without a roof for the middle. It leaves "decent" indeterminate; it makes the conception comprehend more than a single value or group of values, and yet it excludes many values and interests which might ideally belong to the conception of justice. It therefore illustrates both the conflict of this conception of justice with other conceptions of justice, and it is sufficiently loose to include many values and procedures which hang together only partly.

It is suggested that what is involved in Llewellyn's notion of decency is neither bad thinking nor loose expression which critical reflection would correct. It is not the helpless gesture of one who habitually employs sentimental and vague expressions; on the contrary, it is a statement by one who on different themes and problems has a most lively sense for detailed distinctions and exact expressions.[10] Nor is he alone in this result and this tendency. We find similar attitudes in a number of contemporary writers, including, particularly, those who fall near

[10] See, for example, Llewellyn, *On Warranty of Quality and Society* (1936) 36 COLUMBIA LAW REVIEW 699; (1937) 37 COLUMBIA LAW REVIEW 341.

or within the group approaching law empirically and functionally. What unites them is their explicit emphasis on the elasticity, indeterminateness, and ubiquitous relevance of justice.

THE REASONABLENESS OF SATISFACTION

It is in this sense that Nelles is to be understood in his "Toward Legal Understanding."[11] His purpose here is primarily to explain some common confusions about the nature of law and to indicate how the law may be brought closer to its ends.[12] This end, he asserts to be "satisfactoriness to all socially tolerable persons."[13] He elaborates this formula by referring to the presence of a body of ends in any society:

> Whatever the vagueness of justice, natural law, "common right and reason" or whatever it be called, there is always, at every time and place, a considerable body of valuations of particular sorts of conduct in which respectable people approach unanimity.[14]

The clearest equivalent expression of justice he finds to be Bracton's "common warrant of the body politic."[15]

If this conception of justice is taken as a determinative measure of legal activity, it is not only fatally ambiguous but question begging as well. The conception of the "socially tolerable" begs the question because it presupposes a measure of such a group. It is a standard which is hardly relevant to any existing society because it is only on the vaguest principles or on the unimportant details that there is this complete consensus, even if we take the "socially tolerable" to include all citizens. Moreover, it is

[11] (1934) 34 COLUMBIA LAW REVIEW 862, 1041.
[12] *Ibid.*, 862.
[13] *Ibid.*
[14] *Ibid.*, 872.
[15] *Ibid.*

vicious if it be taken to mean the effective voice of any smaller community, since that would mean, in effect, a tyranny either of a majority or of a minority. These criticisms are perfectly apparent and destructive of the conception if it is to be taken as a determinate standard and ideal of law. Actually, Nelles does not so take it, and he is well aware of the difficulties if one seeks to apply it as a touchstone of justice. He feels perfectly free, for example, to use as an equivalent conception that of "reasonableness."

> Bracton's desire that law consist of norms and ways which have "common warrant of the body politic" seems to be the same as we should now express as a desire that law be reasonable or conduce as much as possible and in the best way possible . . . to general convenience.[16]

Nelles indicates clearly that "reasonableness" gives no touchstone. He is of the opinion that judgments of reasonableness are extremely doubtful.

> They may vary with conditions of time and place. Judges, moreover, like other persons, differ in reason and also in prepossessions. And their mores are vague as to the objects at which they should aim. . . . The justice or social expedience of decisions of reasonableness might rarely be disputed if the aim were always Bracton's, and judges were always sensitive to Bracton's touchstone, and could refuse to deal at all with questions about which powerful forces of interest and opinion irreconcilably conflict. But modern conditions have multiplied un-Bractonian judges and hard cases.[17]

In the light of this clear recognition, it should be apparent that Nelles in still holding to the Bractonian "touchstone" has in mind no slide-rule conception of justice. His conception is similar to Llewellyn's in that it is emphasizing the elasticity of the idea of justice. It is used

[16] *Ibid.*, 1044. See 1058.
[17] *Ibid.*, 1059. See 1060, 1071.

by Nelles to stand in opposition to what he calls "Legal Uli," the conception of law as certain, stable, and realizing ends which are themselves clear, known, used, certain, and immutable.[18] Standing opposed to a conception of immutable justice, Nelles's view is not another determinate conception of justice.

> To emphasize the conception of reasonableness and of satisfactoriness to the body politic is not to do away with confusion but to make confusions and problems explicit; if this were done, reasonableness would become an object of study and not a guess.[19]

To emphasize it as a category of ends and standards is to exclude no one standard, even where it is in potential conflict with other ends and measures.

BENEVOLENT JUSTICE

The force of Thurman Arnold's writings depends for their striking effect upon basic confusions concerning the nature and operation of language. His caricatures of legal abstractions, such as law, crime, punishment, and jurisprudences, is often rooted in a misuse of semantics. He implies that if a word has an emotional use and appeal, it therefore has no value as an intellectual instrument; that if a word is not *immediately* referable to experience, it can have no reference to things at all; that because an abstraction is ambiguous, the parts of that ambiguity are likewise ambiguous; that because some abstractions are hypostatized, all abstractions are hypostatizations; that because some abstractions are meaningless and therefore useless for empirical inquiry, only in action and organization is there salvation.

It would not be difficult to apply the same technique of criticism to Arnold's own writing and conceptions. Such

[18] *Ibid.*, 863.
[19] *Ibid.*, 1071.

an approach would be peculiarly successful if applied to his own attempts to state the purpose and standards of social action, such as satisfactoriness to the "respectable citizen," "benevolence," a "practical and humanitarian attitude," "the alleviation of human misery," and "efficiency."[20] Yet such an enterprise would be of little profit for an understanding of his position. For whatever the inadequacy of the technical basis of Arnold's criticism, that criticism is not motivated by an interest in logical clarity alone. The importance of his argument does not depend upon the adequacy of his semantic principles, for his writings are not meant as an illustration of applied semantics and should not be judged on that basis. His chief interest is in a "new creed which can reconcile itself to the facts of human organization."[21] What is required of social ideals is that "they must permit practical institutions to function with security, and provide them with freedom to experiment."[22]

What is needed today is a kind of theory which will be effective as a moral force and as an intellectual playground, yet which will permit politicians to come out of the disreputable cellars in which they have been forced to work.[23]

Arnold is arguing that there must be some expression of the direction of the social enterprise. This he calls a "creed," in other cases a "symbol,"[24] a "dream,"[25] a "ceremony,"[26] and the primary requirement for it is that it shall not interfere with the "practical" efforts to satisfy needs and the experimentation and organization required

[20] The Symbols of Government (1935) 47–48, 89, Chapter X; The Folklore of Capitalism (1937) 169, 387, Chapter XIV.

[21] The Folklore of Capitalism (1937) 391.

[22] The Symbols of Government (1935) 232.

[23] *Ibid.*, 237.

[24] *Ibid.*

[25] The Folklore of Capitalism (1937) 385.

[26] *Ibid.*, 376.

for the realization of those efforts. What this means at the very least is that the only adequate ideal, principle, or standard is one that is sufficiently elastic and indeterminate to permit growth and alteration in both the method of realizing the concrete values the ideal subsumes and in the needs themselves. This view of the purport of Arnold's criticism is supported by his own formulation of "a philosophy for politicians" and his "principles of political dynamics." By "political dynamics" is meant the "science of the diagnosis of maladjusted organizations."[27] Throughout his statement of the principles of the projected science, Arnold presents the problem as having a twofold aspect, one relating to the general formulation of ideals and the other to the practical concrete functions performed by institutions. Individuals, for example, entering an organization are forced "to conform to what is expected of them in terms both of practical results and the representation of sentimental ideals."[28] With respect to the ideals, it is asserted that they must inevitably be "false,"[29] because they can never be adequate to the practical ends and purposes which organizations such as law seek to realize. They can never be adequate because any complex organization will be serving a plurality of purposes which are, or may be, contradictory.[30] Where the ideal becomes solidified sufficiently to be determinate, then it is necessary to reconcile the ideal with the practical results, the reconciliation being accomplished either by ceremony or by splitting the institution into two separate parts, one of which continues the practical activity and the other represents the ideal.[31] But where the ideal and practical needs are not in conflict,

[27] *Ibid.*, 349.
[28] *Ibid.*, 356 (Principle 8).
[29] *Ibid.*, 350 (Principle 2).
[30] *Ibid.*, 357, 376 (Principle 19).
[31] *Ibid.*, 358, 360 (Principles 9, 11).

there the "maximum practical efficiency" is attained,[32] and no social need will be effectively pursued until it gets a formulation of its own.[33] To the extent that any ideal becomes determinate enough to interfere with "common sense actions" which seek to adjust existing functions to new conditions, that ideal is harmful to the institution of which it is the ideal.[34] Now if one asks what these ideals are, apart from or in addition to the anthropological and psychological interpretations which Arnold gives them, the answer would be that they are the "vague aspirations of any group."[35] His view is that present-day creeds do not adequately represent these aspirations, and there is a need for a new formulation of them. Today in the United States we do not have such a formulation, and the closest approach to a symbol of these aspirations is President Roosevelt.[36]

> He [Roosevelt] expresses for the majority of the public the current distrust of old myths and the belief that the Government has a new role to play in providing for security of individuals in their jobs and in the distributions of goods.[37]

By his reference to the psychological need of the public, one might conclude that for Arnold there is no need for an aspiration or a creed for the "politician" or for the "practical reformer." That such is not the case is, however, indicated by the fact that he himself formulates what he believes to be the beginning of an adequate creed for the politician, both as to method and objective; he calls it the "insane asylum approach" to society.[38] It has two phases: to consider the ideals of the people governed "only in the light of their effect on conduct," and "to

[32] *Ibid.*, 376 (Principle 18).
[33] *Ibid.*, 378 (Principle 20).
[34] *Ibid.*
[35] *Ibid.*, 390–91.
[36] *Ibid.*, 390.
[37] *Ibid.*, 391.
[38] THE SYMBOLS OF GOVERNMENT (1935) 232.

make the inmates of the asylum as comfortable as possible."[39] As a statement of an objective, as an aspiration, Arnold calls it the humanitarian point of view.[40] He asserts that this politician's creed will never serve as a general creed for the public because it is too cynical and too destructive of the self-respect of the community and also too simple and direct for the intellectual.[41] Nevertheless, it is adequate for the politician because it expresses "a humanitarian ideal which seems to be indestructible in the march of society—the ideal that it is a good thing to make people comfortable if the means exist by which it can be done."[42] Yet, while it expresses a practical aspiration, it does not restrict the methods nor blind the eye to the practical needs which experience reveals to be the content of that aspiration.[43]

The closing paragraphs of both *The Symbols of Government* and *The Folklore of Capitalism* are, significantly enough, devoted to a plea for an "adult view" of fundamental principles, ideals, and aspirations. The "adult view" is that while we recognize the "practical desirability" of ideals, at the same time it is necessary that we keep them "infinitely elastic" so that "they represent public attitudes and do not strangle public needs"[44] and so that the adherence to these principles does not prevent an adjustment to changing situations nor force the "application of impossible standards to new organizations fumbling about to fill some social need."[45]

[39] *Ibid.*, 233.
[40] *Ibid.*, 232.
[41] *Ibid.*, 236.
[42] *Ibid.* So far as this humanitarian ideal is concerned, it is interesting to note that the myth of present-day public opinion and its symbol (President Roosevelt) differs in no detail from the politician's creed, between which two Arnold draws, in other contexts, the widest contrast. See THE FOLKLORE OF CAPITALISM (1937) 391.
[43] THE SYMBOLS OF GOVERNMENT (1935) 234, 252, 258.
[44] THE FOLKLORE OF CAPITALISM (1937) 392.
[45] *Ibid.*, 293. See THE SYMBOLS OF GOVERNMENT (1935) 269–71.

Arnold arrives at the position which Nelles and Llewellyn have taken. The expressions for justice which these writers use are so used in order to free themselves from strait-jacket conceptions of "proper" methods and aims of law. It is a conscious endeavor on their part to use those expressions which indicate no more than the teleological method of law implied in any criticism or reform of law or any attempt to improve law. It is based on the desire to free law from supposed standards which hamper effective action. It is, however, a position which insists not only that our formulae ought to be worn loosely but also that there is no substantive standard which is determinately usable and at the same time fully adequate and acceptable to all the needs and aims of law.

THE SEARCH FOR JUSTICE

Men have tried to find such a formula, but it is doubtful whether any attempt could be successful. The formal and substantive insufficiencies of the various conceptions have been pointed out from time to time by others but frequently and unfortunately only as a prelude to a further definition.[46] Not only have the conceptions discussed above been utilized in the attempt to arrive at a unifying standard of justice, but the failure of these formulae to satisfy criticism leads to the various other attempts to do the same thing adequately. Consequently, in almost every period of jurisprudence we are able to find a wide variety of competing formulae. There are attempts to locate the standard in terms of distribution according to merit,[47] or

[46] COHEN, ETHICAL SYSTEMS AND LEGAL IDEALS (1933). Part I offers an explicit and straightforward critique of the more favored types. See STAMMLER, THE THEORY OF JUSTICE (1925); TOURTOULON, PHILOSOPHY IN THE DEVELOPMENT OF LAW (1922) Chapter XIV, Section 2; SIDGWICK, THE METHODS OF ETHICS (1884) 262 ff.; COHEN, *Positivism and the Limits of Idealism in Law* in LAW AND THE SOCIAL ORDER (1933). Pound's many discussions of the formulae of justice are valuable because of his interest in understanding the relative emphasis of the different conceptions.

[47] See MARTINEAU, TYPES OF ETHICAL THEORY (1886).

in terms of a standard of distribution according to need. Justice has found its criteria in conformity to custom,[48] in rendering to each individual the opportunity for a realization of his highest self,[49] in regulating conflicts so as to increase the strength of the state,[50] to provide freedom to act and to have, qualified by the like freedom for others.[51] Some definitions have been made in terms of charity, love, equality, or like phrases.[52] Justice defined as so much of morality as judges find it wise to enforce,[53] like most of the other formulae, really begs the question in this case by allocating the problem to another field—assuming such separation of fields to be possible. The question remains, what are the "moral" values? Cardozo, in his efforts to realize justice as a judge, illustrates well enough that values become clarified in law more than in general reflections on values taken as a whole or as a complete system. Cardozo's separation of moral, economic, aesthetic, and legal values is one of the least defensible conceptions he ever attempted to use. Roscoe Pound's statement of his famous engineering conception of law,[54] namely, the effectuating of social interests, has been handled more roughly by friendly and unfriendly critics than it deserves,[55] for its primary emphasis is to express the problem of justice, not the criteria. The "balancing of interests" phrase of Pound is more deserving of criticism, but even here the phrase asserts a problem and ex-

[48] CARTER, LAW, ITS ORIGIN, GROWTH AND FUNCTION (1907).

[49] WILLOUGHBY, SOCIAL JUSTICE (1900).

[50] CARVER, ESSAYS IN SOCIAL JUSTICE (1915).

[51] SPENCER, THE PRINCIPLES OF ETHICS (1892).

[52] See, for example, PATTEE, THE ESSENTIALS OF LAW (1909); LORIMER, THE INSTITUTES OF LAW (1890); SIDGWICK, THE METHODS OF ETHICS (1884); Husserl, *Justice* 47 INTERNATIONAL JOURNAL OF ETHICS 271; Emmett, *Justice and Equality* (1939) 14 PHILOSOPHY 46.

[53] CARDOZO, THE PARADOXES OF LEGAL SCIENCE (1928) 35.

[54] POUND, AN INTRODUCTION TO THE PHILOSOPHY OF LAW (1930) Chapter II.

[55] See COHEN, ETHICAL SYSTEMS AND LEGAL IDEALS (1933) 90; Grossman, *The Legal Philosophy of Roscoe Pound* (1935) 44 YALE LAW JOURNAL 605.

presses a practical conception of what actually occurs, as much at it implies that it is an ideal which carried with it its clear and distinct criteria.

No attempt has been made here to analyze these formulae of justice, but it is suggested that the quantity of written material to be found defining, defending, and criticizing the various formulae without substantial positive results creates a suspicion with regard to the enterprise of definition and with regard to the superiority of one result over the others, especially when the intent has been to give a unifying criterion for law. "Thinkers have complained with justice of the lack of any formula whereby preference can be determined when values are conflicting. There is no common denominator to which it is possible to reduce them."[56] To take this position is, however, not to assert the irrelevance of a teleological attitude toward law. Contemporary empiricism in law, while rejecting the conception of any eternal objective standard directly able to make and to dictate particular principles, does not reject standards nor the need for standards. In this sense, it is completely at one with the attitude expressed by Justinian that justice is "the constant and perpetual will to render each his due," but the emphasis here is upon the "will," the method or enterprise so to speak, not upon "to each his due" if that is taken to be an objective standard. What is "due" each is a problem, not a standard to be used. What is constant is the "will."

ETERNAL JUSTICE

Beginning before Plato and continuing through the years, there is to be found a reference to the absolute and objective standard. Contemporary writing is no exception. "The basis of judgment is objective . . . it is factual, in the real order of things, not fanciful, and not subject to

[56] CARDOZO, THE PARADOXES OF LEGAL SCIENCE (1928) 56–57.

the whims of personal caprice, or the vagaries of shifting custom or public opinion."[57] Until the realist is shown what this "basis" is, he is content to interpret such a statement as a statement of "faith in the better" and of the "pertinence of effort" in law. Even where the locus of that standard is indicated from an empirical point of view, we are faced either with a particular interest which is emphasized or with a general celebration of a faith. This may be illustrated by a consideration of the position taken by Hocking.

Hocking's article, "Ways of Thinking about Rights: a New Theory of the Relation between Law and Morals,"[58] is another attempt to treat a conception of an absolute standard. Hocking believes this standard to be indicated by empirical factors, by certain "hard facts" which a comprehensive study of the law cannot help disclosing. On the basis of these "hard facts," he attempts to suggest something of the role of an absolute ethical standard in law and its development. "A thoroughly realistic study of legal phenomena does not escape the factual influence upon law of the ethical judgments of mankind: on the contrary, this is one of the hardest of hard facts it encounters."[59] The differences as well as the essential agreements between Hocking and the empiricist are brought into prominence when the question is raised as to how this "hard fact" is statable and in what its meaning consists. Primarily, the "fact" consists in this, that not all law is accepted merely in virtue of its existence; while force or sovereign power can make what is "right" in the sense of being an effective right, it cannot make everything right in the sense of being acceptable.[60] Nor do practices or customs justify of themselves that law which expresses and clarifies them. Moreover, there is the "fact" of such activity

[57] Miltner, *Law and Morals* (1934) 10 NOTRE DAME LAWYER 1, 8.
[58] LAW, A CENTURY OF PROGRESS (1937) II, 242.
[59] *Ibid.*
[60] *Ibid.*, 249.

as legal reform.[61] And above all, there is the fact of criticism in law; "it is always pertinent to ask what the law 'ought to be.' "[62]

Hocking expresses these facts in other words, in the language of an "ethical sense." It has become fairly well established, he writes, "that legal and moral principles are not wholly independent of each other,"[63] that men like Jhering, Jellinek, Stammler, and Korkunov in different ways have been trying to define "a positive connection between law and the ethical sense"[64] and at the same time have been trying to "provide law with an ethical steering gear."[65] Hocking also speaks of the facts noted as an illustration of an "*a priori* sentiment," as an illustration of the "influence of the ethical judgments of mankind," and as "a working union of an ethical judgment with a legal rule."[66]

This language is translatable into, and may be seen as a convenient mode of expression for, the empirical matters noted. It could be taken to mean the "hard fact" that law is not per se self sufficient; that law is, and needs to be, evaluated, "reformed"; that law is subject to criticism; that it may always be considered as instrumental; that there is a better and a worse. To say that there is a "union of an ethical judgment with a legal rule," that law has need of an ethical steering gear, would appear to be a convenient way of expressing the fact that law is purposeful. But this language may be used to indicate something more than this, and to this use Hocking does indeed put it.

For the "hard fact" turns out to be more than the fact that the consideration of what ought to be is a poten-

[61] *Ibid.*, 243.
[62] *Ibid.*
[63] *Ibid.*, 242.
[64] *Ibid.*
[65] *Ibid.*
[66] *Ibid.*, 243.

tially present consideration for the evaluation of any given data. It turns out that the ought-to-be that is being discussed is one that is determined solely by the standard of what ought to be when the standard is the "value of valuers," by which he apparently means the worth of the individual as such. It turns out to be something other than the hard fact of criticism; it becomes the hard fact of a specific kind of criticism and the "hard fact" of an absolute standard. The fact, according to Hocking, is that "individuals presume themselves to have rights and further presume these rights to be founded upon a principle of Justice."[67] The fact is one of "individual rights" which are irreducible and which are subject to no instrumental consideration. These latter characterizations of the "hard fact" would appear to make the ethical sense a formative factor operating as a limit presided over by the standard of the "value of valuers" such that, whatever the content of the law, it must not ignore this standard, the intrinsic value of personality, nor what is needed for the "growth of personality."

There is no question that in practical actions there are general moral opinions which formulate and exert pressure upon the practices of a community and which induce obedience. Likewise, it is easily understandable that any procedure which was felt to run violently in opposition to established moral opinions, and which at the same time could not utilize some other moral dictum to balance and offset the first moral maxim, might lead to disregard for the community practice or for the law. Again, there is no serious objection to the attitude that the value of the individual is of importance in the evaluation of going practices. This "hard fact" may well be taken into account by any politician. Further than this, from an instrumentalist point of view, Hocking does not appear

[67] *Ibid.*

legitimately to go. It is only by selection that to ask what ought to be is to ask only or ultimately what ought to be from the standpoint of the "value of valuers." We ask what ought to be from any number of considerations, and one of the "hard facts" of law or of any other social process of evaluation is precisely that the importance of different considerations vary with situations. It is perfectly true, as Hocking points out, the words "public policy" and "efficiency" each by themselves are not sufficient to justify anything. But this applies to his standard as well. Taken in their broadest significance, they all signify merely the need for the possibility of criticism, while taken strictly they offer only one set of possible suggestions for analyzing and criticizing a particular situation, a set which is not homogeneous because "public policy" and "efficiency" are balanced against each other. To make any formula such as the moral sense of the individual not one type of evaluation among others but the absolute and transcendent value to which all others must defer or to which they must refer as instrumental is possible only by making that expression equivalent in meaning to "faith in the better."

NATURAL LAW

In the long history of natural law doctrine wherein are found some of our most serious attempts to define our ends, there is abundant illustration of the fact that the most general and inclusive statements of justice and the good are basically statements of teleological orientation only. Said Thomas Aquinas:

> Consequently the first principle in the practical reason is one founded on the notion of good, *viz., the good is that which all things seek after*. Hence, this is the first precept of law, that *good is to be done and ensued and evil is to be avoided*. All other precepts of the natural law are based on this: so that whatever the practical reason naturally appre-

hends as man's good (or evil) belongs to the precepts of the natural law as something to be done or avoided.[68]

It is clear that this states an orientation of law, a way of looking, and not a standard of particular decision. Thomas Aquinas in his approach to natural law differs in important details considerably from those that preceded him and those that followed him. But what unites most of them is that they state a method and a drive and not a standard in any other sense. Ernest Barker writes of Roman and Stoic natural law:

It is not a body of actual law, which can be enforced in actual courts. It is a way of looking at things—a spirit of "humane interpretation" in the mind of the judge and the jurist—which may, and does, affect the law which is actually enforced, but does so without being actual law itself.[69]

It is this way of "looking at things" that is basic and essential not only for the Romans but for the European tradition.[70] It is this way of looking at things which the realists in law have emphasized in their expressions of justice. The generality of expressions of justice needs to be maintained if it is not to be enslaved to particular ends or methods, which in turn would handicap the legal process and the search for particular goods. "If we would be a slave to that end [namely, the most general] and no other, we would have a guarantee of freedom which we do not now have."[71] In so far as the writers on natural law embodied this aim, there is much in common between them and the contemporary realist writers.

[68] SUMMA THEOLOGICA Part II, First Part, QQ. XC–CXIV; excerpted in HALL, READINGS IN JURISPRUDENCE (1938) 34.

[69] Introduction to GIERKE, NATURAL LAW AND THE THEORY OF SOCIETY (1934) XXXVI.

[70] In many writers on natural law, specific ideals were united to the general conception of *telos*, as with Blackstone, Rutherforth, Burlamaqui, and Locke. Though asserted categorically, criticism finds that logically, and as a matter of fact, these specific ends were hypothetical in character.

[71] Levi, *Natural Law, Precedent and Thurman Arnold* (1938) 24 VIRGINIA LAW REVIEW 587, 611.

CHAPTER VI

THE UNITY OF JUSTICE

MEN in seeking to clarify their ideas about justice have assumed that the quest for the definition of justice is the all important enterprise. The efforts of the philosopher have been justified as an indispensable activity to achieve the indispensable initial clarity of general aims and criteria in law. But if the uses here described are empirically the uses we find the conceptions and expressions of justice to have, then there is ground for asserting that the vitality of justice as a conception used in law derives in good part from its very fluidity and its motive power rather than from its intellectual definition.

The too frequent assumption of philosophers in their attempts to understand justice is expressed by John Stuart Mill:

> Nothing is more indicative of the backward state of speculation than the little progress that has been made respecting the criterion of right and wrong. When we are engaged in pursuit, a clear and precise conception of what we are pursuing would seem to be the first thing we need, instead of the last thing we are to look forward to. A test of right and wrong must be the means . . . of ascertaining what is right or wrong and not a consequence of having attained it.[1]

This demand for an initial clarity is an honorable one, but the necessity or the possibility of attaining to that initial clarity before we act is unrealistic. If such a "test"

[1] UTILITARIANISM (2d ed., 1864) 1 ff.

for purposes were a prerequisite, philosophy itself would be in vain, for philosophers seek rather than exhibit clarity. If, as Woodbridge writes, in a dynamic world a man must run before he can know that he ran, it is no less natural that in a world where action is primary and necessary, men act purposefully before they fully know their purposes; they discover purposes before they know their principles. Here the natural order of events asserts itself. Effective systems in this world are gradual growths and for the most part do not anticipate the details.

It is only to be expected that our formulation of fundamental principles will reflect in part the perplexities that generated their need. The ambiguities and the contradiction of the concrete material remain in the conceptual formulations; the ambiguities of meaning indicate multiplicities of conflicting possibilities. Guesses at the significant character of goods, at what men want or can have, guesses at the importance of varying demands will reflect the conflicting character of these events and possibilities, even though these guesses be nominally reduced to a unified conception. The conception remains unified in words only; a generic idea merely reflects a universe of such universality that violent contradictions can all remain within it and even be regarded as its inherent dialectic.

There is more than a rhetorical distinction in the emphasis on present ills rather than on ideal goods. To assert that justice is problematic implies more than a difference in expression. It implies a distinction which has practical consequences. It may be that evil is evil because the idea of the good is first given. A structural analysis of a given situation that is complete permits such further analysis. Indeed, the conception of justice as the entelechy of the law is a recognition of the fact. But, on the other hand, a functional analysis of the incompleted situation wisely places its emphasis upon present difficulties. Our experience gives us the unknown, the to-be-known-and-acted-upon first, and the known is subsequent to the unknown. This fact a realistic conception of justice would respect by its frank recognition of the relatively indeterminate character of justice. Justice is the consequence of having particular "justices," not the basis for them.

Empirically, our standard of measurement, though not our end, is in a great measure a matter of the quantity of "squeals."[2] It is by complaint that law comes to recognize a problem and hence to seek its solution. Trouble, need, and maladjustment are brought to the attention of law; the law does not seek them out. The adjustments it makes are taken for granted as workable so long as further litigation does not disclose their inadequacies.[3] And under most circumstances the clue afforded by overt complaint is a most valuable tool for remaining sensitive to injustice and for measuring the adequacy of operating laws. "Experiments [in conduct] are to be judged, not *a priori*, but by actually finding, after the fact of their making, how much more outcry or how much appeasement comes about."[4] It is obvious that law and lawmen could prohibit such manifestations of trouble through coercion and through clumsy processes as theologians suppressed heresies on the ground that they were merely expressions of corruption, but that would be like breaking the thermometer in the hope that we thus destroy cold weather. Nor does the democratizing of the legal processes by reducing their costs and extending their range, thus increasing the troubles heard, indicate a fail-

[2] The idiom and the idea of its function were suggested by K. N. Llewellyn.

[3] Cardozo writes: "The rule that functions well has a title deed to recognition."

[4] JAMES, *The Moral Philosopher and the Moral Life* in THE WILL TO BELIEVE (1903) 208.

ure of justice; it can mean only that we have among other things simply made our measures more pervasive and sensitive—like improved techniques for locating disease. Injustice comes before justice and we learn to know justice in proportion to our ability to prevent complaints. These matters have carried insufficient weight in the analyses of our fundamental social principles and even less in our appreciation of the role of the conception of justice in law. We move in extremes, we delude ourselves about the adequacy of our fundamental principles, or we emerge from self-deception only to denounce the use of such principles altogether; we ignore the problem created by a given situation, and, from our position of learned ignorance, we proceed to a forgetful ignorance and bury ourselves in facts and descriptions or, by ignoring the problem, assume ourselves to have solved it. On the other hand, philosophers make it their business to become aware of the confusions in our fundamental principles, but the "initial" clarity they offer as a cure turns out to be verbal; they act as though one could like a magician pull initial clarities out of simple abstractions cultivated in the armchair of our studies.

To the question of what justifies the values which compose justice, it suffices to give an empirical answer. Neither the idea of justice nor the formulae of that idea do so; its concrete justification is not a matter of philosophy but of legal action. The concrete legal situation involves, as a part of that situation, a context of competing values which are for the time being matters of justice. The dialectic is undoubtedly present in this situation which will, if followed, lead us to a "self-justifying" ideal, but once we arrive at this point, we have a justification in terms of a standard which is unknown, one at which both Hocking and Urban arrive.[5] Despite the fact that

[5] HOCKING, LAW AND RIGHTS (1926) 47 ff.; URBAN, VALUATION, ITS NATURE AND LAWS (1909).

the idealist so frequently comes to this position, self-justification is in fact little more than a verbal expression for no-justification-needed.

If justice is the objective of society viewed in legal perspective, then its substantive definition would be a complete statement of all the objectives, all the solutions to conflicts of competing interests and ways. Its definition cannot stop short of indicating all possible objectives and methods, and any principle or set of principles which claim to do so will be found to operate symbolically, and their instrumental value turns upon their indicative, formative, and celebrative functions. Formulae of justice in a sense "justify" values, but values need justification only as they enter law. A just claim, for example, is a need brought to the attention of law and, if recognized as such, becomes a member or part of justice on good behavior and *de facto*. Though formulae of justice may be seen to be implied in evaluative judgments made in law, no judgment is deducible from them.

So comprehended, it becomes an affair of indifference whether we formulate our conception of justice in terms of reason, equality, merit, peace, or security, provided only that from any such conception one may "derive" suggestions for the solution of particular controversies. As soon as we define these various conceptions, we find that they cease to be adequate to all we mean by justice; they begin to be particular legal standards. It makes little difference whether we define justice as simply the administration of declared law and then introduce another term, such as "equity" (in its ethical meaning), to cover what we have not included in our narrow definition or whether we bring it all under the term justice. The precise formulation is of no importance for a concept of justice functioning within the operations of a going society, if only there is some expression which recognizes the fact that law is purposefully oriented or concerned with interests which it seeks to further or to evaluate. As Morris Cohen said:

> More recently, some students of political theory have come to recognize that the essence of natural rights is . . . the appeal to an ideal to which law should conform. Certainly . . . some appeal from it [the law] to natural law, political or public morality, or the principles of sound social policy and public welfare—*call* it what you will—is unavoidable.[6]

Law cannot be understood apart from this search for the better law, though law need not necessarily be understood solely in those terms. The idea of justice in its broadest sense is the expression of this teleological orientation. The more one studies the process of law the more apparent "the energies within the legal system—what the ancients called its 'entelechy'—are revealed in all their vigor."[7] That is, justice is a symbol for the recognition that law is not given but is constantly being made. The principles of justice do not represent the assumptions of law, blueprints for court decisions, nor criteria to be appealed to as legal grounds; they express inadequacies and possibilities; they direct by encouraging or discouraging, not by discovering; they are necessary incentives in cases of failure and also celebrate achievements, solutions. Justice, like good or beauty, is thus not an ordinary idea of reason but a form of practical reason. It is a symbol of a need for further refinement.

An idea whose function it is to stand for or represent a kind of context and a kind of approach, a generic characteristic of legal action, an idea whose function is limited to represent the need for and the possibility of the better, an idea that symbolizes the fundamental effort to relieve complaint is not a mere device or rhetorical gesture. Yet when generic normative expressions are used as

[6] *Jus Naturale Redivivum* (1926) 25 PHILOSOPHICAL REVIEW 761, 775.
[7] CARDOZO, THE PARADOXES OF LEGAL SCIENCE (1928) 19.

definitions or standards of what the better is or of what a complaint is, they become "devices." There is a real place and function for *obiter dicta,* of which judges are more aware than lawyers. From time to time there must be an expression more or less emotional of the judge's orientation. An awareness of complaint and a desire to relieve complaint of its occasion need some sort of expression. But the symbol of the desire for the better, it should be remembered, does not mean the presence of the principles or methods which will relieve complaint.

The conception of justice may be viewed from two perspectives. Justice is the answer to the question, "What ought to be law?" but it is more importantly the question itself. From the point of view of the end, justice is the answered question, but from an empirical approach and from the point of view of the present situation, justice is the question and the continuous questioning.[8] This formative aspect is what gives to justice its power and its ubiquitous relevance. As the eternal question, it is a continuous prod to the asking and the answering of questions. As a question, it is the reminder of the hypothetical character of aims, and a reminder as well of the importance of constant criticism and evaluation. If value is a symbol for "what ought to be" in general, it is evident that for practical purposes some limiting field ought to be indicated for law. Justice performs this function, relating values to the ideal of judgment.

The idea of justice is at heart, then, the idea of legal criticism. It functions as the symbol of criticism in and for law. The fact that the idea of justice expresses the critical and evaluative factors in the consideration of laws makes it basic in orienting the personnel of law to the fact of the need for constant criticism. Law as an integral

[8] Levi, *Natural Law, Precedent, and Thurman Arnold* (1938) 24 VIRGINIA LAW REVIEW 586; see also 596: "The analysis [in terms of justice or natural law] raises eternal questions; it does not solve them."

part of going communities, indeed as one of the most essential structural factors in them, requires a sensitivity to the fact that it is a structural aspect of moving, developing communities, that it participates rather than constitutes. Justice in its generic character expresses the need for constant adaptation of law to the patterns and processes of the groups and the institutions of which law is a partial articulation. It serves as a constant reminder of the fact that law operates as the public instrument of adjustments, not merely of law to other activities but of activity to activity.

Justice states the fundamental method of law—the method of purposeful activity, that is, action directed towards ends. Law is teleological, and justice in its broadest terms is the statement of that fact and is in a sense the instrument which keeps law teleological in its method. It is the formal symbol for both the entelechy of law and law's effort to realize its ends. Any appeal beyond the present law is intelligible because law is teleologically oriented; justice expresses and celebrates this purposeful orientation of law; it is formative because its use keeps men sensitive to their responsibility and willing to fight for concrete achievements. It thus is the expression for the motive power of law most generally expressed. The efforts men make to realize ends through law illustrate the fact of social teleology. This striving toward the better is the enterprise of justice. It is why justice as a conception in terms of which men clothe specific goods and sought adjustments is formative, celebrative. Justice is the motive power of law; it will continue to be so as long as it retains its fluidity and remains generically a symbol of the better in law. In the language of Justinian, "justice is the set and constant purpose to render everyone his due," but "what is due to everyone is not laid down concretely; it has to change from time to time; the only thing that ought to be certain and inflexible is the purpose."[9]

If justice finds its most general meaning to be the effort to develop possibilities inherent in law, then justice as a criterion of legal action will be such only when legal action itself becomes ideal. Speaking in Platonic figures, the sun of justice cannot be seen directly but only as it is reflected in the clouds of hope and prophecy that assume the hypothetical shapes of man's visions as man succeeds in making better law. Justice is like the Delphian oracle; it speaks vaguely. It says "seek"; it does not say "seek this." It commands society to build; it does not direct height, size, or number; it gives no specification. The latter is a matter of art, of sensitivity to what is needed and of intelligence with respect to what is possible.

An investigation into normative problems, whether analytical or empirical, is not itself normative, though it may affect evaluation as a consequence of the investigation and though normative interests may even be the motive of the undertaking. An inquiry into the traits of justice is, however, not an inquiry into what the law ought to seek, do, or refrain from doing. Its purpose is not to forge a general standard or standards of the ideal of law, nor is it an effort to state what the ideal of law ought to be. What has been said of the ideal of law is a statement of what the activity of a consummate ideal is in law—its power, limitations, and general traits as revealed in the legal and, more especially, the judicial process.

The traits of justice may now be briefly summarized. Justice exhibits a radical pluralism and multiplicity with respect to its ends and standards; just adjustments, as these concretely come to be and to be used in the process

[9] Wu, *The Juristic Philosophy of Roscoe Pound* (1923) 18 ILLINOIS LAW REVIEW 285, 303.

of decision, are not readily definable. Justice denotes a class whose members are partly unified, partly autonomous, partly in overt competition, and both potentially and actually in conflict even though nominally their conflicts be transcended by symbolic mergers. The contents of justice have life histories and are dynamic, and for that reason the contents may be said to have a temporal dimension. The concepts of justice are hypothetical, and no part of justice is self-evidently just but may always be called upon to justify itself. The role of particular, clear, and distinct values, ends, and standards is to guide and illumine judgment determinately, but in constantly occurring and important phases of legal judgment, justice is problematic and an object of search; while in much of the judicial process, just decisions are practical compromises and adjustments. By nature, principles of justice are manipulated rather than followed in reaching decisions. In the constantly altering content of justice there are to be found general ends and standards, mostly procedural in character, such as impartiality and the values associated with it. Because of their relevance to phases of any third-party judgment they are universal and relatively permanent. They do not, however, sum up or unify the total conception of justice, and they may even be at times sacrificed. No one standard or end exhausts the content of justice or gives it a substantive unity. Formulae which attempt to express the unity of justice or attempt to establish an order of priority among the parts operate neither as standards nor ends. In their practical functioning, they express the need for specific illumination rather than provide the illumination needed. They are valuable not because they integrate but because they are elastic. They become bearers of specific, sought values, and their utility rests in their mediating services to social and legal needs and values. Such, for example, is their service as gateways for as yet legally unrecognized values, as bridges between the old and the new, as mediators in the problem of flux and permanence, as organizers of group sympathy, as stimulants to wider criticism. The power of justice in law and the relevance of justice at all times to the judicial process is seen to lie not in its intellectual definition but in its motive power; for the idea of justice is the entelechy of law. In its widest and most enduring sense, justice is the teleological aspect of law. It is, however expressed, the insistence that law is the means to ends, making achievement, realization, preservation, and constant criticism always relevant to judgment.

SELECTIVE BIBLIOGRAPHY

SELECTIVE BIBLIOGRAPHY

I. REALISTIC JURISPRUDENCE

Arnold, T. W. Apologia for Jurisprudence (1935) 44 Yale Law Journal 729–53.

——— Criminal Attempts—the Rise and Fall of an Abstraction (1929) 40 Yale Law Journal 53.

——— The Folklore of Capitalism. New Haven, 1937.

——— The Folklore of Mr. Hook—a Reply (1938) 5 University of Chicago Law Review 349–55.

——— The Jurisprudence of Edward S. Robinson (1937) 46 Yale Law Journal 1282–89.

——— Law Enforcement—an Attempt at Social Dissection (1932) 42 Yale Law Journal 1–24.

——— Restatement of the Law of Trusts (1931) 31 Columbia Law Review 800.

——— Review of L. Green, *Judge and Jury* (1930) 40 Yale Law Review 833.

——— The Role of Substantive Law and Procedure in the Legal Process (1932) 45 Harvard Law Review 617–47.

——— The Symbols of Government. New Haven, 1935.

——— Trial by Combat and the New Deal (1933) 47 Harvard Law Review 913.

Beutel, F. K. Some Implications of Experimental Jurisprudence (1934) 48 Harvard Law Review 169–97.

Bingham, J. W. Legal Philosophy and the Law (1914) 9 University of Illinois Law Review 98–119.

——— The Nature of Legal Rights and Duties (1913) 12 Michigan Law Review 1–26.

——— Science and Law (1913) 25 Green Bag 162–70.

——— What Is the Law? (1912) 11 Michigan Law Review 1, 109.

Cairns, H. Law and Anthropology (1931) 31 Columbia Law Review 32–56.

——— Law and the Social Sciences. New York, 1935.

——— Theory of Legal Science (1937) Maryland State Bar Association Reports 62–71.

——— Valuation of Legal Science (1940) 40 Columbia Law Review 1–13.

Cantor, N. Law and the Social Sciences (1930) 16 American Bar Association Journal 385–91.

Chafee, Z., Jr. Some New Ideas about Law (1936) 11 Indiana Law Journal 503–23.

Clark, E. E. The Complaint-Allegations in Particular Actions (1927) 5 North Carolina Law Review 101–24.

——— History, Systems, and Functions of Pleading (1926) 5 American Law School Review 716–34.

——— Relations, Legal and Otherwise (1922) 5 University of Illinois Law Quarterly 26–35.

——— The Restatement of the Law of Contracts (1931) 42 Yale Law Review 363.

Cohen, F. S. Ethical Basis of Legal Criticism (1931) 41 Yale Law Journal 201.

——— Ethical Systems and Legal Ideals. New York, 1933.

——— Modern Ethics and the Law (1934) 4 Brooklyn Law Review 33–50.

——— Problems of Functional Jurisprudence (1937) 1 Modern Law Review 15–26.

——— Transcendental Nonsense and the Functional Approach (1935) 35 Columbia Law Review 809–41.

Cook, W. W. Act, Intention and Motive in the Criminal Law (1916) 26 Yale Law Journal 645–63.

——— "Facts" and the "Statements of Facts" (1937) 4 University of Chicago Law Review 233–46.

——— Law and the Modern Mind: a Symposium (1931) 31 Columbia Law Review 82–115.

——— Scientific Method and Law (1927) 13 American Bar Association Journal 303.

——— Substance and Procedure in the Conflict of Law (1932) 42 Yale Law Review 358.

——— Tort Liability and the Conflict of Laws (1935) 35 Columbia Law Review 202–28.

——— Williston on Contracts (1939) 33 Illinois Law Review 497–516.

Corbin, A. L. Conditional Delivery of Written Contracts (1926) 36 Yale Law Journal 443–63.
——— Contracts for the Benefit of Third Persons (1931) 46 Law Quarterly Review 12–45.
——— The Law and the Judges (1914) 3 Yale Law Journal 234.
——— Legal Analysis and Terminology (1919) 29 Yale Law Journal 163–73.
——— Mr. Justice Cardozo and the Law of Contracts (1939) 39 Columbia Law Review 57–87.
——— Rights and Duties (1924) 33 Yale Law Journal 501–27.
Corwin, E. The Constitution as Instrument and as Symbol (1936) 30 American Political Science Review 1071–85.
——— The "Higher" Law Background in American Constitutional Law (1929) 42 Harvard Law Review 365–409.
——— The Schechter Case—Landmark or What? in Law, a Century of Progress, 1835–1935. 3 vols. New York, 1937. II, 32–81.
——— The Twilight of the Supreme Court. New Haven, 1934.
Douglas, W. O., and D. S. Thomas. The Business Failures Project—a Study in Methodology (1930) 39 Yale Law Journal 1013; (1931) 40 Yale Law Journal 1034.
Finkelstein, M. The Functional View of Legal Liability (1924) 34 International Journal of Ethics 243–353.
Frank, J. Law and the Modern Mind. New York, 1930.
——— Mr. Justice Holmes and Non-Euclidean Legal Thinking (1932) 17 Cornell Law Quarterly 568–603.
——— Realism in Jurisprudence (1934) 7 American Law School Review 1057–76.
——— Save America First. New York, 1938.
——— Some Realistic Reflections on Some Aspects of Corporate Reorganization (1931) 19 Virginia Law Review 541, 698.
——— What Courts Do in Fact (1932) 24 Illinois Law Review 645–66, 761–84.
Frank, L. K. Institutional Analysis of Law (1924) 24 Columbia Law Review 480–99.
Frankfurter, F. The Conditions for and the Aims and Methods of Legal Research (1930) 6 American Law School Review 663.
——— Law and Politics. New York, 1939.

Frank, J. (*Cont.*) Mr. Justice Holmes and the Supreme Court. Cambridge, Mass., 1938.

——— The Public and Its Government. New Haven, 1930.

——— Reconstruction and the Law (1932–33) New Hampshire Bar Association Reports 73–104.

Goble, G. W. Law as a Science (1934) 9 Indiana Law Journal 294–313.

——— Negative Legal Relations Re-Examined (1922) 6 Illinois Law Quarterly 36.

——— A Redefinition of Basic Legal Terms (1935) 35 Columbia Law Review 535–47.

——— Sanction of a Duty (1928) 37 Yale Law Journal 426–44.

Green, L. Judge and Jury. Kansas City, 1930.

Hale, R. L. Commissions, Rates, and Policies (1940) 53 Harvard Law Review 1103–44.

——— The "Fair Value" Merry-Go-Round, 1898-1938 (1939) 33 Illinois Law Review 517–31.

——— Force and the State: a Comparison of "Political" and "Economic" Compulsion (1935) 35 Columbia Law Review 149–201.

——— Legal Factors in Economic Society. 2d ed., mimeographed. 2 vols. 1937.

——— Our Equivocal Constitutional Guarantees (1939) 39 Columbia Law Review 563–94.

——— Rate Making and the Revision of the Property Concept (1922) 22 Columbia Law Review 209.

——— Some Challenges to Conventional Legal Views (1923) 9 American Bar Association Journal 330.

——— Unconstitutional Conditions and Constitutional Rights (1935) 35 Columbia Law Review 321.

——— Value and Vested Rights (1927) 27 Columbia Law Review 523–29.

——— What is a "Confiscatory" Rate? (1935) 35 Columbia Law Review 1045–52.

Hall, J. Theft, Law and Society. Boston, 1935.

Hamilton, W. H. The Path of Due Process of Law, in The Constitution Reconsidered. Edited by C. Read. New York, 1938. Pages 167–91.

——— Preview of a Justice (1939) 48 Yale Law Journal 819.

Hamilton, W. H., and D. Adair. Power to Govern. New York, 1937.

Hamilton, W. H., *et al.* Price and Price Policies. New York, 1938.

Harper, F. V. Forms of Law and Moral Content (1927) 22 Illinois Law Review 259–73.

——— Law in Action and Social Theory (1930) 40 International Journal of Ethics 305–29.

——— The Pragmatic Process in Law (1931) 41 International Journal of Ethics 305–28.

——— Some Implications of Juristic Pragmatism (1929) 39 International Journal of Ethics 269–90.

Hutcheson, J. C., Jr. Judging as Administration (1934) 7 American Law School Review 1057–76.

——— Judgment Intuitive. Chicago, 1938.

——— Law as Liberator. Chicago, 1937.

——— Lawyer's Law and the Little, Small Dice (1932) 7 Tulane Law Review 1–12.

——— This Thing Men Call Law (1934) 2 University of Chicago Law Review 1–13.

Isaacs, N. How Lawyers Think (1923) 23 Columbia Law Review 555–63.

——— The Law and the Facts (1922) 22 Columbia Law Review 1–13.

——— "The Law" and the Law of Change; Tentative Study in Comparative Jurisprudence (1917) 65 University of Pennsylvania Law Review 665–79, 748–63.

——— Schools of Jurisprudence; Their Places in History and Their Present Alignment (1918) 31 Harvard Law Review 373–411.

Jaffin, G. H. Prologue to Nomostatics (1935) 35 Columbia Law Review 1–32.

Keyser, C. J. Nature of the Doctrinal Function and Its Role in Rational Thought (1932) 41 Yale Law Journal 713–44.

——— On the Study of Legal Science (1929) 38 Yale Law Journal 413–22.

Landis, J. S. Administrative Process. New Haven, 1938.

Lerner, M. Constitution and Court as Symbols (1937) 46 Yale Law Journal 1290–1319.

Levy, B. H. Cardozo and the Frontiers of Legal Thinking. New York, 1938.

——— Law a Dynamic Integration (1936) 5 Brooklyn Law Review 417–52.

Litchman, M. M. The Application of the Theory of Relativity to Law (1932) 6 Temple Law Quarterly 311–31, 515–51.

——— Four Modern Philosophies and Their Application to Law (1931) 5 Temple Law Quarterly 215–34.

Llewellyn, K. N. Across Sales on Horseback (1939) 52 Harvard Law Review 725–46.

——— Behind the Law of Divorce (1932) 32 Columbia Law Review 1281–1308; (1933) 33 Columbia Law Review 249–94.

——— The Bramble Bush. New York, 1930.

——— Case Law, in Encyclopedia of the Social Sciences.

——— Cases and Materials on the Law of Sales. Chicago, 1930. Introduction.

——— The Conditions for and the Aims and Methods of Legal Research, in Handbook of the Association of American Law Schools. 1929. Page 35.

——— The Constitution as an Institution (1934) 34 Columbia Law Review 1.

——— Contract-Institutional Aspects, in Encyclopedia of the Social Sciences.

——— Legal Tradition and Social Science Method—a Realist's Critique, in Essays on Research in the Social Sciences. Washington, 1931.

——— The Normative, the Legal, and the Law Jobs: the Problem of Juristic Method (1940) 49 Yale Law Journal 1355–1401.

——— On Philosophy in American Law (1934) 82 University of Pennsylvania Law Review 205–12.

——— On Reading and Using the New Jurisprudence (1940) 26 American Bar Association Journal 300–307.

——— On Warranty of Quality and Society (1936) 36 Columbia Law Review 699; (1937) 37 Columbia Law Review 341.

——— Our Case Law of Contract: Offer and Acceptance (1938) 48 Yale Law Journal 1–37, 497–527.

——— Präjudizienrecht und Rechtsprechung in Amerika. Leipzig, 1933.

——— A Realistic Jurisprudence—the Next Step (1930) 30 Columbia Law Review 431–65.

——— The Rule of Law in Our Case Law of Contract (1938) 47 Yale Law Journal 1243–72.

——— Some Realism about Realism—Responding to Dean Pound (1931) 44 Harvard Law Review 1222–64.

——— Through Title to Contract and a Bit Beyond (1938) 15 New York University Law Quarterly Review 159–209.

Lorenzen, E. G., E. H. Phelps, and R. J. Heilman. The Restatement of the Conflict of Laws (1935) 83 University of Pennsylvania Law Review 555–89.

Moore, U. An Institutional Approach to the Law of Commercial Banking (1928) 38 Yale Law Journal 703.

Moore, U., and G. Sussman. The Lawyer's Law (1932) 41 Yale Law Journal 566–76.

——— The Rational Basis of Legal Institutions (1923) 23 Columbia Law Review 609.

Moore, U., G. Sussman, and E. Corstvet. Drawing against Uncollected Checks (1935) 45 Yale Law Journal 1–38, 260–92.

Morris, C. How Lawyers Think. Cambridge, Mass., 1937.

Nelles, W. Commonwealth v. Hunt (1932) 32 Columbia Law Review 1128.

——— Toward Legal Understanding (1934) 34 Columbia Law Review 862–89, 1041–75.

Oliphant, H. Current Discussions of Legal Methodology (1921) 7 American Bar Association Journal 241–43.

——— Facts, Opinions, and Value-Judgments (1932) 10 Texas Law Review 127–39.

——— The Public and the Law, the Three Major Criticisms of the Law and Their Validity (1932) 18 American Bar Association Journal 787–93.

——— The Return to Stare Decisis (1928) 14 American Bar Association Journal 71, 159.

Patterson, E. W. Can Law Be Scientific? (1930) 25 Illinois Law Review 121–47.

——— Cardozo's Philosophy of Law (1939) 88 University of Pennsylvania Law Review 71–91, 156–76.

——— Pragmatism as a Philosophy of Law, in The Philosopher of the Common Man. New York, 1940.

——— The Restatement of the Law of Contracts (1933) 33 Columbia Law Review 397–427.

——— Scope of Restitution and Unjustified Enrichment (1936) 1 Missouri Law Review 223–36.

Phillips, P. G. A Lawyer's Approach to Commercial Arbitration (1934) 44 Yale Law Review 31.

Pickett, C. Nicknames and Unfair Competition (1935) 35 Columbia Law Review 33–62.

Powell, T. R. Law as a Cultural Study (1917) 4 American Law Review 330–38.

Radin, M. The Chancellor's Foot (1935) 49 Harvard Law Review 44–67.

——— The Courts and Administrative Agencies (1935) 23 California Law Review 469–81.

——— The Education of a Lawyer (1937) 25 California Law Review 676–92.

——— A Juster Justice, a More Lawful Law, in O. K. McMurray, Legal Essays. Edited by M. Radin and A. M. Kidd. Berkeley, 1935.

——— The Law and Mr. Smith. New York, 1938.

——— Law as Logic and Experience. New Haven, 1940.

——— Legal Realism (1931) 31 Columbia Law Review 824–28.

——— Permanent Problems of the Law (1929) 15 Cornell Law Quarterly 1–24.

——— A Restatement of Hohfeld (1938) 51 Harvard Law Review 1141–64.

——— Scientific Method and the Law (1931) 19 California Law Review 164–72.

——— The Theory of Judicial Decision (1925) 11 American Bar Association Journal 357.

Robinson, E. S. Law and the Lawyers. New York, 1935.

Rothschild, J. L. Men and Law; a Lawyer's View of the Judicial Process (1932) 1 Brooklyn Law Review 1–27.

Sussman, G., and S. R. Gamer. Standards and Grades of Quality for Foods and Drugs (1935) 2 University of Chicago Law Review 578–99.

Tolin, L. The Role of Penalties in Criminal Law (1928) 37 Yale Law Journal 1048–69.

Ulman, J. N. A Judge Takes the Stand. New York, 1933.

Wu, J. C. H. Essays in Jurisprudence and Legal Philosophy. Shanghai, 1930.

——— Realistic Analysis of Legal Concepts (1932) 5 China Law Review 1.

Yntema, H. E. The Antecedents of Examination before Trial in New York (1934) 34 Columbia Law Review 831.

——— Constitutional Principles and Jurisprudence (1937) 25 Georgetown Law Journal 577–606.

——— The Hornbook Method and the Conflict of Laws (1927) 37 Yale Law Journal 468.
——— Implications of Legal Science (1933) 10 New York University Law Quarterly Review 279–310.
——— Legal Science and Reforms (1934) 34 Columbia Law Review 207–29.
——— The Purview of Research in the Administration of Justice (1931) 16 Iowa Law Review 337–60.
——— Rational Basis of Legal Science (1931) 31. Columbia Law Review 925–55.

II. CRITICISM AND EVALUATION OF LEGAL REALISM

Adler, M. Law and the Modern Mind—Legal Certainty (1931) 31 Columbia Law Review 91.
Ayres, C. E. Review of F. Cohen, *Ethical Systems and Legal Ideals* (1932) 43 Yale Law Journal 158.
Bohlen, J. H. Review of J. Frank, *Law and the Modern Mind* (1931) 79 University of Pennsylvania Law Review 822.
Cardozo, B. N. Address (1932) 55 New York State Bar Association Reports 263–307.
Cohen, M. R. A Critical Sketch of Legal Philosophy in America, in Law, a Century of Progress, 1835–1935. 3 vols. New York, 1937. II, 266–320.
——— Justice Holmes and the Nature of Law (1931) 31 Columbia Law Review 352.
Dickinson, J. Legal Rules and the Process of Decision (1931) 79 University of Pennsylvania Law Review 833.
——— Legal Rules; Their Application and Elaboration (1931) 79 University of Pennsylvania Law Review 4052.
Fowler, R. L. The New Philosophies of Law (1914) 27 Harvard Law Review 718–31.
Friedrich, C. J. Remarks on Llewellyn's View of Law, Official Behavior, and Political Science (1935) 50 Political Science Quarterly 419–31.
Fuller, L. L. American Legal Realism (1934) 82 University of Pennsylvania Law Review 429–62.
Goodhart, A. L. Some American Interpretations of Law, in Modern Theories of Law. Edited by W. I. Jennings. 1933.

Hook, S. "The Folklore of Capitalism" (1928) 5 University of Chicago Law Review 341–49.

——— Neither Myth nor Power—a Rejoinder (1939) 5 University of Chicago Law Review 356.

Hutchins, R. Autobiography of an Ex-Law Student (1934) 7 American Law School Review 105.

Jones, J. W. Modern Discussions of the Aims and Methods of Legal Science (1931) 47 Law Quarterly Review 62–91.

Kantorowicz, H. Some Rationalism about Realism (1934) 43 Yale Journal 1240–53.

Kennedy, W. B. Functional Nonsense and the Transcendental Approach (1936) 5 Fordham Law Review 272–300.

——— Men or Laws (1932) 2 Brooklyn Law Review 11–26.

——— More Functional Nonsense: a Reply to Felix S. Cohen (1937) 6 Fordham Law Review 75–89.

——— New Deal in the Law (1934) 68 United States Law Review 533–39.

——— Pragmatism as a Philosophy of Law (1924) 9 Marquette Law Review 63.

——— Principles or Facts? (1935) 4 Fordham Law Review 53–71.

——— Realism, What Next? (1938) 7 Fordham Law Review 203.

Kocourek, A. (1913) 9 Illinois Law Review 138.

Lerner, M. The Shadow World of Thurman Arnold (1938) 47 Yale Law Journal 687–703.

Levi, E. H. Natural Law, Precedent and Thurman Arnold (1938) 24 Virginia Law Review 584–612.

Marx, M. Juristischer Realismus in den Vereinigten Staaten von Amerika (1936) 10 Revue Internationale de la Théorie du Droit, No. 1.

Pound, R. The Call for a Realistic Jurisprudence (1931) 44 Harvard Law Review 697–711.

——— Fifty Years of Jurisprudence (1937) 50 Harvard Law Review 557–82; (1938) 51 Harvard Law Review 444–72, 777–812.

Radbruch, G. Anglo-American Jurisprudence through Continental Eyes (1936) 52 Law Quarterly Review 530–45.

Sullivan, J. L. Speculation of Thurman W. Arnold (1938) 1 Polamerican Law Journal 3.

III. CONTEMPORARY JURISPRUDENCE

Aguanno, G. d'. Die Ideale der Gerichtigkeit in der modernen Gesellscheft (1909–10) 3 Archive für Rechts und Wirtschaftsphilosophie 69–78, 221–40.

Albertsworth, E. F. Need for New Premises in the Law (1922) 56 American Law Review 17–38.

Allen, C. K. Precedent and Logic (1925) 41 Law Quarterly Review 329–45.

——— Jurisprudence—What and Why? (1930) 42 Juridical Review 275–302.

——— Legal Duties and Other Essays in Jurisprudence. Oxford, 1931.

Alvarez, A. New Conceptions and New Bases of Legal Philosophy (1918) 13 Illinois Law Review 167–82.

Ames, J. B. Law and Morals (1908) 22 Harvard Law Review 97–113.

Amos, M. S. Some Reflections on Philosophy of Law (1927) 3 Cambridge Law Journal 31–41.

Aumann, F. R. Some Changing Patterns in Legal Order (1935) 24 Kentucky Law Journal 38–57.

Basu, K. The Modern Theories of Jurisprudence. Calcutta, 1925.

Bentley, A. F. Process of Government. Chicago, 1908.

Bocobo, J. The Cult of Legalism (1937) 17 Philippine Law Journal 253–63.

Brandeis, L. D. Living Law (1916) 10 Illinois Law Review 461–71.

Brown, W. J. Underlying Principles of Modern Legislation. 3d ed. London, 1914.

Burgess, J. W. The Sanctity of Law. Boston, 1927.

Cardozo, B. N. The Growth of Law. New Haven, 1924.

——— The Jurisdiction of the Court of Appeals. New York, 1903.

——— A Ministry of Justice (1921) 35 Harvard Law Review 113–26.

——— The Nature of the Judicial Process. New Haven, 1922.

——— The Paradoxes of Legal Science. New York, 1928.

Carter, J. C. Law; Its Origin, Growth, and Function. New York, 1907.

Carver, T. N. Essays in Social Justice. Cambridge, Mass., 1915.

Cohen, M. R. Jus Naturale Redivivum (1926) 25 Philosophical Review 761–77.

——— Law and the Social Order. New York, 1933.

——— Moral Aspects of the Criminal Law (1940) 49 Yale Law Journal 987–1027.

——— On Absolutisms in Legal Thought (1936) 84 University of Pennsylvania Law Review 681–715.

——— Reason and Nature. New York, 1931.

Commons, J. R. Problem of Correlating Law, Economics and Ethics (1932) 8 Wisconsin Law Review 3–26.

Coudert, F. R. Certainty and Justice. New York, 1913.

Del Vecchio, G. The Homo Juridicus and the Inadequacy of Law as a Norm of Life (1937) 11 Tulane Law Review 503–26.

——— Justice, droit, état; études de philosophie juridique. Paris, 1938.

Dewey, J. Logical Method and Law (1924) 10 Cornell Law Quarterly 17–27.

——— Nature and Reason in Law (1914) 25 International Journal of Ethics 25–32.

Dickinson, J. Administrative Justice and the Supremacy of Law in the United States. Cambridge, 1927.

——— The Law behind Law (1929) 29 Columbia Law Review 113–46, 285–319.

Dietze, H. H. Naturrecht in der Gegenwart. Bonn, 1936.

Drake, J. H. Rule of Law and the Legal Right (1921) 19 Michigan Law Review 365–82.

——— Sociological Interpretation of Law (1918) 16 Michigan Law Review 599–616.

Duguit, L. Objective Law (1921) 21 Columbia Law Review 17.

Duncan, J. L. The End and Aim of Law (1935) 47 Juridical Review 157; (1938) 50 Juridical Review 256.

Ehrlich, E. Fundamental Principles of the Sociology of Law. Translated by W. L. Moll. Cambridge, Mass., 1939.

——— Sociology of Law (1922) 36 Harvard Law Review 130–45.

Emmett, D. E. Justice and Equality (1939) 14 Philosophy 46–59.

Ferson, M. L. Nature of Law and Rights (1927) 1 University of Cincinnati Law Review 154–83.
Foulke, R. R. The Philosophy of Law. Philadelphia, 1925.
Freund, E. Standards of American Legislation. Chicago, 1917.
Fuller, L. L. Legal Fictions (1930) 25 Illinois Law Review 363, 513, 877.
Goodhart, A. L. Essays in Jurisprudence and the Common Law. Cambridge, 1931.
——— Law and the State (1931) 47 Law Quarterly Review 118–40.
Grossman, W. L. The Legal Philosophy of Roscoe Pound (1935) 44 Yale Law Journal 605.
——— Notes on an Ethical Philosophy of Law (1936) 5 Brooklyn Law Review 160–71.
Haines, C. G. The Law of Nature in State and Federal Decisions (1916) 25 Yale Law Journal 617–57.
——— The Revival of Natural Law Concepts. Cambridge, Mass., 1930.
Hankin, G. Ethics and Law (1923) 33 International Journal of Ethics 416–35.
Hardman, T. P. Stare Decisis and the Modern Trend (1926) 32 West Virginia Law Quarterly 163–91.
Harris, R. C. Idealism Emergent in Jurisprudence (1936) 10 Tulane Law Review 169–87.
Hill, O. A. The Natural Law (1925) 13 Georgetown Law Journal 367.
Hocking, W. E. Lasting Elements of Individualism. New Haven, 1937.
——— Present Status of the Philosophy of Law and of Rights. New Haven, 1926.
——— Ways of Thinking about Rights: a New Theory of the Relation between Law and Morals, in Law, a Century of Progress, 1835–1935. 3 vols. New York, 1937. II, 242–66.
Holmes, O. W., Jr. Collected Legal Papers. New York, 1921.
——— The Common Law. Boston, 1938.
Hughes, W. T. Immutable Principles of Legislation (1909) North Dakota Bar Association Reports 138–76.
Hummel, T. Einfuhrung in das Gerechtigkeitsproblem (1926) 29 Archive für systematiche Philosophie 82–91.

Husserl, G. Justice (1937) 47 International Journal of Ethics 271–307.
Jenks, E. The Function of Law in Society, in Society of Comparative Legislation and Comparative Law. 3d Series. 1923. Vol. V, Part IV, p. 176.
——— The New Jurisprudence. London, 1933.
Jennings, I. A Plea for Utilitarianism (1938) 2 Modern Law Review 22.
Keeton, G. W. The Elementary Principles of Jurisprudence. London, 1930.
Kelsen, H. Pure Theory of Law: Its Method and Fundamental Concepts (1934) 50 Law Quarterly Review 474–98; (1935) 51 Law Quarterly Review 517–35.
Kermack, S. G. Utility of Legal Philosophy (1925) 3 New York Law Review 353–56.
Kinkead, E. B. Jurisprudence, Law and Ethics. 1908.
Kocourek, A. An Introduction to the Science of Law. Boston, 1930.
——— Legal Duties (1939) 23 Temple University Law Quarterly 151–65.
——— The Nature of Interests and Their Classification (1917) 23 American Journal of Sociology 359–68.
——— Subjective and Objective Elements in Law (1927) 31 Illinois Law Review 687–703.
Konvitz, M. R. Utilitarian Justice: Technical and Discretionary (1931) 40 Philosophical Review 67–78.
Krabbe, H. The Modern Idea of the State. New York, 1913.
Le Buffe, F. P., and J. V. Hayes. Jurisprudence. New York, 1936.
Lepaulle, O. Function of Comparative Law, with a Critique of Sociological Jurisprudence (1922) 35 Harvard Law Review 838–58.
London School of Economics. Modern Theories of Law London, 1933.
Mecham, F. R. Inquiry Concerning Justice (1916) 14 Michigan Law Review 361–82.
Mecham, P. Jurisprudence of Despair (1936) 21 Iowa Law Review 669–72.
Miller, W. G. The Data of Jurisprudence. London, 1903.
Miltner, C. C. Law and Morals (1934) 10 Notre Dame Lawyer 1–10.

Mitchell, E. T. Social Ideals and the Law (1937) 46 Philosophical Review 113–31.
Moody, R. A. Law and Morality (1939) 51 Juridical Review 323–43.
Moor, J. Das Problem des Naturrechts (1935) 28 Archive für Rechts und Sozialphilosophie 325–47, 543–69.
Parsons, F. Legal Doctrine and Social Progress. New York, 1911.
Pattee, W. S. The Essential Nature of Law. Chicago, 1909.
Patten, S. H. The New Jurisprudence (1913) 62 University of Pennsylvania Law Review 1–16.
Peters, F. Vom Problem der Gerechtigkeit. Jena, 1930.
Pollock, F. Essays in Jurisprudence and Ethics. London, 1882.
——— Essays in the Law. London, 1922.
——— First Book of Jurisprudence. London, 1923.
Pound, R. A Comparison of Ideals of Law (1933) 47 Harvard Law Review 1–17.
——— Courts and Legislation (1913) 7 American Political Science Review 361–83.
——— Do We Need a Philosophy of Law? (1905) 5 Columbia Law Review 339.
——— The End of Law as Developed in Juristic Thought (1914) 27 Harvard Law Review 195–234, 605–28; (1917) 30 Harvard Law Review 201–25.
——— How Far Are We Attaining a New Measure of Values in Twentieth-Century Juristic Thought? (1936) 42 West Virginia Law Quarterly 81–95.
——— Ideal and Actual in Law—Forty Years After (1933) 1 George Washington Law Review 431–47.
——— Ideal Element in American Judicial Decision (1931) 45 Harvard Law Review 136–48.
——— Individualization of Justice (1938) 7 Fordham Law Review 153.
——— An Introduction to the Philosophy of Law. New Haven, 1930.
——— Jurisprudence, in Encyclopedia of the Social Sciences.
——— Justice According to Law (1913) 13 Columbia Law Review 698–713; (1914) 14 Columbia Law Review 1–26, 103–21.
——— Law and Morals. 2d ed. Chapel Hill, 1926.

Pound, R. (*Cont.*) Law and the Science of Law in Recent Theories (1934) 43 Yale Law Journal 525–36.

——— Law in Books and Law in Action (1910) 44 American Law Review 12–44.

——— Legal Rights (1915) 29 International Journal of Ethics 92–116.

——— Making Law and Finding Law (1916) 82 Central Law Journal 351–59.

——— Mechanical Jurisprudence (1908) 8 Columbia Law Review 605–23.

——— Modern Trends in Jurisprudence: a Symposium—Law and the Science of Law in Recent Theories (1934) 7 American Law School Review 1057–75.

——— The Need for Sociological Jurisprudence (1907) 19 Green Bag 607–15.

——— Outlines of Lectures on Jurisprudence. 3d ed. Cambridge, Mass., 1930.

——— The Philosophy of Law in America (1913–14) 7 Archive für Rechts und Wirtschaftsphilosophie 213–23, 385–400.

——— The Scope and Purpose of Sociological Jurisprudence (1911) 24 Harvard Law Review 591–619; (1912) 25 Harvard Law Review 140–68, 489–516.

——— Social Justice and Legal Justice (1912) 75 Century Law Journal 455–63.

——— Some Implications of Recent Legislation (1939) 45 West Virginia Law Quarterly 205–19.

——— Theories of Law (1912) 22 Yale Law Journal 114–50.

——— Theory of Judicial Decision (1923) 36 Harvard Law Review 641–62, 802–25, 940–59.

——— A Theory of Social Interests (1921) 15 Papers and Proceedings of the American Sociological Society 16.

——— Twentieth-Century Ideas as to the End of Law, in Harvard Legal Essays Written in Honor of and Presented to Joseph Henry Beale and Samuel Williston. 1934. Pages 357–75.

Robson, W. A. Civilization and the Growth of Law. London, 1935.

Rottschaeffer, H. Jurisprudence: Philosophy or Science? (1927) 11 Minnesota Law Review 292, 298–305.

Smith, G. H. Logic, Jurisprudence and the Law (1914) 48 American Law Review 801–39.

——— Review of Current Theories of Jurisprudence (1909) 43 American Law Review 821–51.

Smith, T. V. The American Doctrine of Equality in the Light of Evolutionism (1925) 35 International Journal of Ethics 377–403.

——— The Transcendental Derivation of Equality in America (1925) 35 International Journal of Ethics 164–88.

Stammler, R. Fundamental Tendencies in Modern Jurisprudence (1923) 21 Michigan Law Review 623–54, 765–85, 862–903.

——— The Idea of Justice (1923) 71 University of Pennsylvania Law Review 303–17.

——— The Theory of Justice. Translated by J. Husek. New York, 1925.

Stone, H. J. Law and Its Administration. New York, 1924.

Stowell, F. M. The Modern Conception of Justice (1908) 19 International Journal of Ethics 44–60.

Taylor, H. The Science of Jurisprudence (1909) 22 Harvard Law Review 241–49.

Thilly, F. Sociological Jurisprudence (1923) 32 Philosophical Review 373–84.

Tourtoulon, P. de. Philosophy in the Development of Law. Translated by M. McRead. New York, 1922.

Valentine, G. D. Doubts regarding the Foundations of Jurisprudence (1925) 37 Juridical Review 57–70, 142–61, 350–69.

Vinje, A. J. Present Day Problems in Jurisprudence (1926) 60 American Law Review 448–64.

Vinogradoff, P. Aims and Methods of Jurisprudence (1924) 24 Columbia Law Review 1–7.

——— Common Sense in Law. New York, 1914.

——— Crisis of Modern Jurisprudence (1920) 29 Yale Law Journal 312–20.

——— Foundations of a Theory of Rights (1924) 34 Yale Law Journal 60–69.

——— Historical Jurisprudence. 2 vols. London, 1923.

——— Legal Standards and Ideals (1924) 23 Michigan Law Review 108.

Warsoff, L. Equality and the Law. New York, 1938.

Wilde, N. The Meaning of Rights (1924) 34 International Journal of Ethics, 283–97.

Williston, S. Change in the Law (1935) 69 United States Law Review 237–42.

——— Some Modern Tendencies in the Law. New York, 1929.

Willoughby, W. W. Social Justice. New York, 1900.

Winfield, P. H. Ethics in English Case Law (1931) 45 Harvard Law Review 112.

Woods, C. A. Changing Conceptions of Justice (1921) 7 American Bar Association Journal 101–6.

Wright, C. A. An Extra-Legal Approach to Law (1932) 10 Canadian Bar Review 1–17.

INDEX

INDEX

Bei Fragen zur Produktsicherheit wenden Sie sich bitte an:
If you have any questions regarding product safety,
please contact:

Walter de Gruyter GmbH
Genthiner Straße 13
10785 Berlin
productsafety@degruyterbrill.com